I0401366

Contents

Foreword

In today's dynamic and fiercely competitive business landscape, where margins are shrinking and customer expectations are soaring, effective supply chain management has evolved from a mere advantage to an absolute necessity. From ensuring a steady flow of raw materials, optimizing inventory levels, to delivering products swiftly and cost-effectively to customers, every link in the supply chain plays a pivotal role in creating value and fostering customer satisfaction.

However, mastering the intricate art of supply chain management is no easy feat. It demands seamless coordination between various departments within an organization, from procurement and production to warehousing, sales, and marketing. It requires a deep understanding of market dynamics, the ability to anticipate demand fluctuations, and the skill to negotiate effectively with partners across the supply chain. Any misstep or inefficiency can trigger a domino effect, leading to increased costs, lost revenue, and a tarnished reputation.

This book aims to equip you with the knowledge and tools needed to navigate the complexities of supply chain management and emerge victorious. Through 19 comprehensive chapters, we will embark on a journey to explore the key facets of this critical business function, unraveling its intricacies and illuminating its potential for driving growth and profitability.

We will delve into the core principles of inventory management, guiding you on how to optimize stock levels, minimize carrying costs, and avoid the pitfalls of stockouts and overstocks. We'll explore strategies for enhancing supply chain efficiency, from selecting the right suppliers to managing transportation and distribution networks. We'll also equip you with the skills to negotiate effectively with partners and build lasting, mutually beneficial relationships.

In today's digital age, technology plays an increasingly vital role in supply chain management. We'll delve into how you can leverage cutting-edge tools and solutions, from inventory management software to data analytics and artificial intelligence, to gain real-time visibility into your supply chain, make informed decisions, and proactively address potential disruptions.

Furthermore, we'll address the critical aspect of risk management, exploring strategies to mitigate risks associated with supply chain disruptions, demand fluctuations, and other unforeseen events. By building resilience into your supply chain, you can ensure business continuity and protect your bottom line.

Through real-world examples, case studies, and expert insights, we'll bring these concepts to life, demonstrating their practical application and impact on businesses across various industries. Whether you're a seasoned supply chain professional, a budding entrepreneur, or simply someone seeking to understand this critical business function, this book will serve as a valuable resource, providing you with the knowledge and tools to navigate the complexities of supply chain management and achieve sustainable success.

Join us on this enlightening journey as we unravel the mysteries of supply chain management and empower you to transform your supply chain into a source of competitive advantage and a catalyst for growth.

Le Van De

Entrepreneur from Vietnam

Chapter 1: Top Five Don'ts of Inventory Management and Supply Chain Optimization

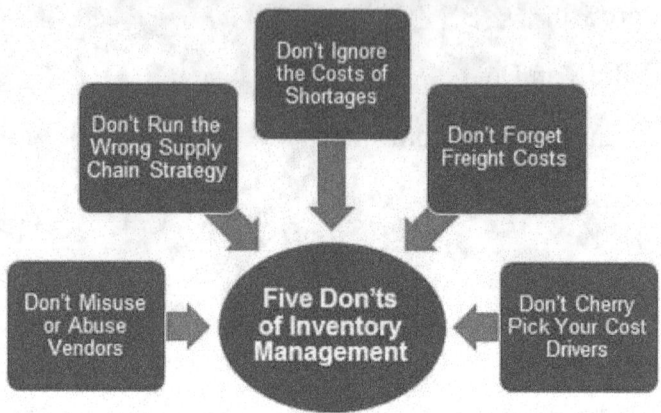

In 2014, a major disruption shook the consumer electronics industry. A leading smartphone manufacturer faced a severe chip shortage due to an unexpected snowstorm in Texas, the location of their main chip manufacturing plant. As a result, millions of phones couldn't be produced on time, causing delays in new product launches and billions of dollars in losses. This event starkly highlighted the critical importance of effective inventory management and supply chain optimization.

Some companies have a firm grasp on managing their inventory. Their entire supply chain is geared towards reaping the benefits of collaborative efforts. Vendors are treated as partners, inventory strategies are aligned, stockouts and shortages are minimized, freight costs are under control, and the company clearly defines its inventory holding costs relative to the costs of not having inventory. Sounds pretty simple, doesn't it? For some companies, it is; for others, it isn't.

So, why do some companies excel at optimizing their supply chain while others continue to fall short? Ultimately, the answer lies in avoiding the five don'ts of inventory management.

These simple rule-sets are essential guidelines. They will simplify how your company views and manages the inventory needed to win business while helping you define all your cost drivers for more informed decision-making.

1. Don't Misuse or Abuse Vendors

There will always be corporate buyers and inventory managers who believe the best way to interact with vendors is through aggression. These buyers are never their vendor's top priority. They are the procurement professionals who hop from one vendor to the next, oblivious to the impact and consequences of their actions.

Vendors should be treated as partners. When you misuse, abuse, or disrespect a vendor, you leave them no choice but to treat you as nothing more than an opportunistic sale – and when they make that sale, you can be sure you'll pay for it.

It's often during emergencies or rush orders that buyers suddenly realize the consequences of their actions. However, do you blame the vendor, or do you pause and understand that your actions and approach to business forced their hand? In many cases, it's not even the salesperson's decision to take action, but rather the management they report to that decides how to proceed. The vendor won't forget how you've behaved in the past, and management may compel the salesperson to seek some measure of revenge when you finally come calling with that crucial emergency.

Example: A furniture manufacturing company consistently pressures its wood supplier for price reductions and expedited deliveries without considering the supplier's capabilities. When the company needs a rush order of wood to complete a major project, the supplier refuses, leading to costly delays and damage to the company's reputation with clients.

2. Don't Run the Wrong Supply Chain Strategy

Sure, we'd all love to run Just-in-Time (JIT). We'd all love to lower our capital costs, eliminate issues related to damage and theft, avoid obsolescence, lower insurance costs, and eliminate a plethora of inventory cost drivers. JIT is so appealing because it means carrying just enough inventory to meet our backlog.

JIT minimizes inventory counts, reduces financing needs, and allows companies to better manage payables and receivables. However, few enterprises can make it work as intended.

If you have a limited product offering and substantial sales volumes across that offering, then maybe JIT works for your company. However, customer demand for your products must be consistent and linear. If you know you'll get an order in a given quarter but are unsure which week or month, or if you're sure you'll get that yearly contract but aren't sure which quarter it will happen in, then maybe JIT isn't for you.

Focus on one simple rule for supply chain optimization: Match your inventory strategies to your customers' needs, your market's business cycles, and your product's sales cycles. If that means running Min-Max or a demand-driven derivative, so be it. Just don't run something you can't simply because someone else is.

Explanation of Terms:

- **Just-in-Time (JIT):** An inventory management strategy where goods are received only as they are needed for production or sale, minimizing storage costs and increasing efficiency.

- **Min-Max:** An inventory control system where minimum and maximum inventory levels are set for each item. When inventory reaches the minimum level, a new order is placed to replenish it to the maximum level.

- **Push-Pull:** A supply chain strategy combining elements of both "push" (production based on forecasts) and "pull" (production based on actual demand).

Example: A fast-fashion retailer could use a Push-Pull strategy, where they produce a base quantity of popular items based on forecasts (push) while also producing additional items based on specific customer requests (pull).

3. Don't Ignore the Costs of Shortages or Out-of-Stock (OOS) Situations

It's easy to assume a company saves money when its inventory counts are low. After all, we're not tying up capital in inventory, and we're not risking obsolete products or damage, right? It seems logical. However, the costs of not having inventory can be just as high as having too much.

Instead of focusing on the costs of holding inventory, consider the risks of not having it. First, you'll miss out on sales and lose the potential profit. Second, you might lose a customer who prefers to deal with your competition. Third, you could lose more than just that one customer, potentially sacrificing a valuable portion of your market share.

Let's assume you don't lose that sale. What are the costs of a stockout on your business? The answers are simple. First, you'll have to expedite orders to your warehouse, a significant cost. Second, you'll incur overtime in manufacturing and shipping. Finally, you'll end up paying for freight on your customer's late order. In the end, shortages cost money, and you must understand the costs of out-of-stock situations.

Example: A grocery store runs out of milk on a weekend, forcing customers to go elsewhere. This not only leads to immediate lost sales but could also cause customers to switch to a competitor in the future.

Input Total Inventory Value on Hand (Monthly Basis)		$ 750,000.00

Inventory Holding Costs		Total
Cost of Money: Let's assume your yearly interest rate on loans and credit lines is 5%. This yearly interest rate can be transferred to a daily interest rate. Since you use money to purchase inventory, every day you hold inventory is a direct cost to your company.	5%	$ 37,500.00
Ruined Inventory: These are parts and materials that are damaged beyond repair. This is because of poor handling methods inside the warehouse. This happens frequently when inventory is not properly packaged and stored.	3%	$ 25,000.00
Electricity Costs: These are costs relating to lighting, and general electricity. It can also include the cost to keep the warehouse cool in the summer, and warm in the winter.	3%	$ 20,000.00
Lost Customers: It's common to lose customers because you did not have the inventory available, or the inventory you delivered was damaged. Very few companies track lost customers because of poor inventory management practices.	3%	$ 20,000.00
High Freight Costs: These costs occur when you have to pay expedited freight to rush parts and materials in because your inventory was low, or the inventory you did have, was damaged. This is also includes those times when you have to rush product to your customers because you didn't maintain a proper inventory count. *** Include an amount above and beyond your standard per-unit freight cost on incoming parts and raw materials.	7%	$ 50,000.00
Overtime: This is when your company pays overtime for employees to either receive, or ship out products. Again, this happens when you don't have the inventory available when it's needed and must therefore rush parts & materials into your warehouse.	3%	$ 20,000.00
Damaged Inventory: The more inventory is handled, the more likely damage will occur. This often happens when you have to move slow moving inventory to a new location in your warehouse to make room for faster selling products.	7%	$ 50,000.00
Dead Stock, Obsolete Inventory & Theft: These are parts that can not be sold because there is no use for them anymore. They can be considered obsolete or outdated products. In this case, they can only be sold for scrap. Included in this cost is the cost of theft.	7%	$ 50,000.00
Total Yearly Inventory Holding Costs	**36%**	**$ 272,500.00**

4. Don't Forget Freight Costs

Isn't it baffling how we look at projected gross profit margins on sales, only to be confronted with the reality that our projected numbers don't match the actuals? It happens all the time, typically in companies that ignore their freight costs.

These companies always purchase at the last minute. They're afraid to hold inventory, operating so lean that they're constantly expediting incoming raw materials and finished goods. They lack a solid understanding of market demand. Finally, they fail to track their freight costs back to their source.

Instead of assigning freight costs to each unit purchased, these companies lump that cost into a miscellaneous account. At the end of the month or quarter, they tally their supposed profit and then reconcile these hidden costs. Only then does their profit inexplicably decline.

Example: A toy manufacturer frequently incurs high freight costs to quickly import materials from overseas due to underestimating demand. These additional freight costs significantly reduce the company's profit margins.

5. Don't Cherry-Pick Your Cost Drivers

Don't focus solely on the costs you understand while ignoring those you don't. The best enterprises recognize it's a balancing act. They know the cost of keeping products on their shelves and the cost of not having them. There are two costs at play, and both must be understood.

Tracking these costs isn't impossible. Understanding your cost drivers for holding inventory involves tracking all your individual holding costs. Meanwhile, you can measure the costs of shortages and stockouts by tracking overtime, defining the costs of poor handling due to rush shipments, tracking expedite fees, aggregating surcharges from vendors for rush orders, and defining freight costs in and out of the warehouse to fulfill late customer orders.

Every company needs inventory. We might complain when we have too much, but we regret it when we don't have enough. Finding that balance involves tracking all costs and then designating someone as the inventory asset manager, responsible for balancing the sales team's demands for more inventory against procurement's desire to reduce it.

Example: An electronics component distributor focuses solely on reducing inventory holding costs, neglecting the shipping costs incurred from having to expedite deliveries to customers when stockouts occur. This leads to higher overall operating costs and impacts profitability.

Conclusion

Effective inventory management and supply chain optimization are vital for maintaining profitability and competitiveness. By avoiding the five "don'ts" outlined above, you can minimize costs, improve customer service, and ensure your business always has enough inventory to meet market demand. Remember, inventory management isn't just about controlling the quantity of goods in your warehouse; it's also about building partnerships with suppliers, choosing the right strategies, and comprehensively tracking costs. By applying these principles, you can transform inventory management from a potential liability into a strategic asset for your business.

Chapter 2: B2B Purchasing Negotiation: Five Strategies to Reduce Vendor Prices

Picture this: You're a procurement manager, tasked with securing the best possible deal for your company. Across the table sits a seasoned salesperson, armed with persuasive tactics and a mandate to maximize their profit. The negotiation begins, and the stakes are high. Every dollar saved translates to increased profit margins for your company. But how do you navigate this high-pressure situation and emerge victorious?

In my sales career, I've encountered countless buyers who excelled at negotiation. Some possessed a natural talent, while others honed their skills through practice and perseverance. The most successful negotiators combined an innate ability to reduce prices with a relentless drive to secure the best terms. Now, I'm turning the tables and sharing their secrets.

Here are five cost-cutting negotiation strategies that purchasing professionals have used against me in my business development career. These strategies are straightforward, easy to implement, and guaranteed to lower your company's costs.

1. Don't Broadcast Your Needs too Soon

Purchasing managers who prematurely reveal their flexibility or eagerness for a deal often find themselves at a disadvantage. Asking for a discount right off the bat allows the salesperson to adjust their offer later, potentially leaving money on the table. Seasoned procurement professionals understand this and avoid making this mistake. They know when and how to utilize their concessions, never revealing their hand too early.

- Focus on establishing the initial price and hold back your concessions. Secure a starting point and then strategically introduce your requests, gradually chipping away at the price or terms.

- Don't show your cards too early. Only when the salesperson believes the negotiation is nearing its end should you start leveraging your most valuable concessions to further drive down the price.

Example: Imagine you're negotiating the purchase of a new software system. Instead of immediately asking for a discount, focus on understanding the full scope of the offering and its value to your company. Once the salesperson presents their initial price, you can then begin to introduce your requests, such as additional features, extended support, or, of course, a price reduction.

Additional Insights:

- **Understanding the Power of Information:** In any negotiation, information is power. By withholding your needs initially, you maintain an information advantage. The salesperson may make assumptions about your budget or priorities, potentially leading them to offer concessions you hadn't even considered.

- **The Art of Timing:** Timing is critical in negotiation. Introducing your concessions too early can make them seem less valuable. By waiting until the salesperson believes the deal is almost closed, you create a sense of urgency and increase the likelihood of them making further concessions to seal the deal.

- **Building Trust:** While it's important to be strategic, avoid being deceitful or manipulative. Building trust with the salesperson is essential for long-term relationships. Be transparent about your goals and constraints, and work collaboratively to find a mutually beneficial solution.

2. Don't Make a Threat You Can't Back Up

Empty threats are easily spotted by experienced salespeople. Some procurement professionals are unaware of how often they resort to threats, either consistently throughout a single negotiation or repeatedly in the buyer-seller relationship.

Making threats you don't intend to follow through on only breeds complacency in the salesperson. Your goal is to ensure they're constantly striving to earn your business. You want them to consistently offer competitive pricing to secure future orders.

- Be prepared to act on your threats if the salesperson fails to respond. This will not only make them take your words more seriously but also encourage them to offer better pricing in the future. Keeping them on their toes prevents them from taking your business for granted.

Example: If you threaten to switch suppliers unless the salesperson offers a better price, be prepared to actually do so if they don't meet your expectations. This demonstrates your seriousness and motivates the salesperson to work harder to retain your business.

Additional Insights:

- **The Importance of Credibility:** Your credibility as a negotiator is crucial. If you make empty threats, the salesperson will quickly learn to ignore them, undermining your negotiating power.

- **Focus on Alternatives:** Before entering a negotiation, identify alternative suppliers or solutions. This strengthens your position and gives you leverage if the current negotiation doesn't progress as desired.

- **Use Threats Sparingly:** Threats should be a last resort, not a primary tactic.

Overusing threats can damage relationships and create a hostile negotiating environment.

3. Match High-Value Concessions with High-Value Concessions

Prioritize your concessions before entering any negotiation. This allows you to match a high-value request from the salesperson with one of your own.

- Create a list of your high-value concessions. When the salesperson makes a significant request, counter with one of equal value. Don't end the negotiation if they can't grant a specific concession; be persistent and move on to the next high-value item on your list. You're bound to find one they'll accept.

- Develop your concession list using a "what if" strategy. Consider potential scenarios and identify concessions you'd be willing to make in exchange for specific benefits from the salesperson.

Example: If the salesperson asks for a larger upfront payment, you could counter by requesting a longer warranty period or additional training sessions.

Additional Insights:

- **Understanding Value:** Not all concessions are created equal. Identify the concessions that are most valuable to you and the salesperson. This allows you to make strategic trades that benefit both parties.

- **The Power of Reciprocity:** People are naturally inclined to reciprocate. By offering a concession, you increase the likelihood that the salesperson will feel obligated to offer one in return.

- **Don't Give Away Too Much:** While it's important to be flexible, avoid giving away too much too soon. Hold back some concessions for later in the negotiation to maintain leverage.

4. Add a Personal Touch

It's not uncommon for purchasing and sales departments to view each other with animosity. After all, they have opposing goals. This conflict can sometimes lead to confrontational negotiations. Avoid falling into this trap.

- Explain to the salesperson that you have strategic initiatives to achieve. Outline your goals and objectives, and be open about the pressures you face.

- Adding a personal touch to the negotiation fosters a free exchange of ideas. Reaching a successful agreement is challenging, if not impossible, when both parties are unwilling to engage on a level playing field.

- Adopt a less adversarial approach. Be straightforward about your needs and explain why they're important. Strive to understand the salesperson's position and ask them to understand yours. Like you, they have constraints and limitations. Adding a personal touch might disarm them and make them more receptive to your requests.

Example: Share a brief story about how a cost reduction would benefit your team or the company as a whole. This helps the salesperson see beyond the numbers and understand the human impact of the negotiation.

Additional Insights:

- **Building Relationships:** B2B relationships are often long-term. Building rapport and establishing a positive connection with the salesperson can lead to more favorable outcomes in future negotiations.

- **Active Listening:** Pay attention to the salesperson's verbal and nonverbal cues.

This will help you understand their needs and concerns, allowing you to tailor your approach and find mutually beneficial solutions.

- **Finding Common Ground:** Look for areas of shared interest or goals. This can help create a collaborative atmosphere and facilitate a win-win outcome.

5. Keep Your Vendors Honest

Complacency is as detrimental to purchasing as it is to sales. You might believe you have the ideal vendor—competitive pricing, excellent terms, and timely deliveries. But if you're not up-to-date on market pricing or unaware of the latest offers, how can you be certain you're getting the best deal? You can't. That's why it's crucial to keep your vendors on their toes by demonstrating your market knowledge.

- Market pricing is dynamic. Salespeople are more proactive when they know you're well-informed. Let them know you're in tune with the market; it might even prompt them to offer a price concession early in the negotiation.

Example: Casually mention a recent competitor offer or industry trend during the negotiation. This signals to the salesperson that you're not easily swayed and encourages them to put their best foot forward.

Additional Insights:

- **Regular Market Research:** Stay informed about market trends, competitor pricing, and new technologies. This knowledge empowers you to negotiate from a position of strength.

- **Request Quotes from Multiple Vendors:** Don't rely solely on your incumbent supplier. Regularly solicit quotes from other vendors to ensure you're getting the best possible value.

- **Leverage Your Buying Power:** If you're a large buyer or have the potential for repeat business, use that leverage to negotiate better terms and pricing.

Conclusion

You don't have to be a born negotiator to secure the best deals. You just need to be willing to learn. Define the constraints you're working within, outline your acceptable outcomes, and always be prepared with a list of concessions you need and some you're willing to grant. Having a clear picture of your ideal outcome will streamline the negotiation process.

Remember, successful negotiation is a combination of strategy, preparation, and effective communication. By implementing these five tactics and continuously refining your skills, you can consistently achieve favorable outcomes for your company and build stronger, more mutually beneficial relationships with your vendors. Negotiation is not just about winning or losing; it's about finding solutions that work for everyone involved. By approaching negotiations with a collaborative mindset and a focus on creating value, you can achieve sustainable success in your procurement efforts.

Remember, the key to effective negotiation lies in preparation

Chapter 3: Five B2B Cost-Cutting Supply Chain Strategies: Unlocking Hidden Profits

Introduction: The Hidden Power of Supply Chain Optimization

In the fast-paced, competitive arena of modern business, the pursuit of profit is an endless endeavor. Companies are constantly seeking innovative strategies to boost their margins and outmaneuver their rivals. While a proactive sales team armed with sharp negotiation skills can certainly drive revenue, there exists another, often underestimated, path to profitability: supply chain optimization. The supply chain, the intricate network that orchestrates the flow of goods and services from raw materials to the end customer, holds immense potential for cost reduction and profit maximization. A well-oiled supply chain can streamline operations, minimize waste, and enhance customer satisfaction, all of which contribute to a healthier bottom line. In this chapter, we'll delve into five powerful B2B cost-cutting supply chain strategies that any company can implement to unearth hidden profits and fuel sustainable growth.

Before we embark on our exploration of these strategies, let's pause to grasp the true cost of an inefficient supply chain. Imagine a bustling manufacturing plant where production lines grind to a halt due to a shortage of a critical component. The silence is deafening, the workers are idle, and every minute of downtime translates into lost revenue and missed deadlines. Or envision a warehouse overflowing with slow-moving inventory, tying up valuable capital and incurring storage costs that eat into profit margins. These scenarios, while all too common, illustrate the financial drain that supply chain inefficiencies can cause. A study by the Harvard Business Review revealed that companies with highly efficient supply chains can achieve profit margins up to 7.5% higher than their competitors. This staggering statistic serves as a wake-up call for businesses that have yet to harness the power of supply chain optimization. By proactively addressing inefficiencies and implementing cost-cutting measures, businesses can not only boost their bottom line but also enhance their overall competitiveness. They can improve customer satisfaction by ensuring timely deliveries and reducing stockouts, free up capital to invest in innovation and expansion, or other strategic initiatives. And they can create a more agile and resilient supply chain that can adapt to changing market conditions and customer demands.

Strategy 1: Consignment Inventory - Turning Inventory into a Cash Flow Asset

Consignment inventory is a strategic partnership between a buyer and a supplier where the supplier retains ownership of the inventory until it's sold by the buyer. This model allows the buyer to maintain optimal stock levels without the upfront financial burden of purchasing inventory. It's a win-win situation: the buyer benefits from improved cash flow and reduced carrying costs, while the supplier gains increased product visibility and potential sales.

Month	Consignment Inventory (Customer's Location)	Customer's Usage	Vendor's Ownership of Consignment
1	1000	0	1000
2	900	100	900
3	800	100	800
4	550	250	550
5	250	300	250
6	0	250	0

Benefits of Consignment Inventory

- **Improved Cash Flow:** Consignment inventory frees up working capital, allowing businesses to invest in other areas or reduce debt. This can be particularly beneficial for small businesses or those operating in industries with long sales cycles, where tying up capital in inventory can strain cash flow and limit growth opportunities.

- **Reduced Inventory Carrying Costs:** The buyer avoids costs associated with storing and managing inventory that hasn't yet been sold. This includes expenses like warehouse rent, utilities, insurance, and the risk of obsolescence or damage. By shifting the responsibility of inventory ownership to the supplier, the buyer can significantly reduce their carrying costs and improve their financial efficiency.

- **Mitigated Stockout Risk:** By having readily available inventory, businesses can fulfill customer orders promptly and avoid lost sales due to stockouts. This enhances customer satisfaction and protects market share. In today's competitive landscape, where customers have numerous options, the ability to consistently meet demand is crucial for building loyalty and retaining market share.

- **Lower Freight Costs:** With consignment inventory, the supplier typically manages transportation and logistics, potentially leading to lower freight costs for the buyer. This can be especially advantageous for businesses dealing with bulky or specialized products that require specialized handling or transportation.

Considerations and Risks

While consignment inventory offers numerous benefits, it's essential to be aware of the potential considerations and risks involved:

- **Supplier Relationship:** Consignment inventory requires a high level of trust and collaboration between the buyer and supplier. It's crucial to choose reliable suppliers with a proven track record of inventory management and timely replenishment. Conduct thorough due diligence, establish clear performance expectations, and maintain open communication to ensure a successful partnership.

- **Inventory Management:** While the supplier retains ownership, the buyer still needs to effectively manage and track the consigned inventory to ensure accurate billing and avoid stockouts or overstocks. This requires clear communication channels, robust inventory tracking systems, and regular reconciliation of inventory records.

- **Suitability:** Consignment inventory might not be suitable for all products or industries. It's essential to assess the specific circumstances, such as product perishability, demand variability, and supplier capabilities, before entering into a consignment agreement. Products with short shelf lives, unpredictable demand, or complex handling requirements might not be ideal for consignment inventory.

Real-World Example

A leading electronics retailer partners with a smartphone manufacturer to implement a consignment inventory program for a new flagship phone launch. This allows the retailer to showcase the latest model without the risk of carrying unsold inventory if demand doesn't meet expectations. The manufacturer benefits from increased brand visibility and potential sales through the retailer's extensive network.

Actionable Tips for Implementing Consignment Inventory

- **Supplier Selection:** Carefully select reliable suppliers with a proven track record of inventory management and timely replenishment. Conduct thorough due diligence, including checking references and reviewing their financial stability.

- **Clear Agreements:** Establish clear and comprehensive consignment agreements that outline the terms and conditions, including inventory levels, replenishment schedules, carrying cost sharing, liability for damaged or lost goods, and procedures for returning unsold inventory.

- **Technology and Communication:** Utilize inventory management software and other technology solutions to track inventory levels, automate replenishment orders, and facilitate real-time data sharing with the supplier. Maintain open communication channels with the supplier to address any issues or concerns promptly.

- **Regular Reviews:** Conduct periodic reviews of the consignment inventory program to assess its effectiveness, identify areas for improvement, and make necessary adjustments to the agreement.

Strategy 2: Vendor Consolidation - Streamlining Your Supplier Network

In the intricate web of supply chain management, the number of vendors a company works with can significantly impact its efficiency and cost structure. Vendor consolidation involves strategically reducing the number of suppliers a company purchases from, consolidating purchases with fewer, more strategic partners.

The Power of Consolidation

Vendor consolidation offers a multitude of benefits for businesses seeking to optimize their supply chain and reduce costs. By consolidating purchases with fewer vendors, businesses can leverage their buying power to negotiate volume discounts, lower prices, and reduced administrative overhead. This can lead to significant cost savings across the supply chain, freeing up resources for other strategic initiatives.

Moreover, consolidating with fewer suppliers allows for deeper relationships and greater collaboration. This can lead to improved communication, better service levels, and joint problem-solving to address any supply chain challenges. By working closely with a select group of trusted suppliers, businesses can foster a sense of partnership and mutual benefit, leading to long-term value creation.

Another advantage of vendor consolidation is the simplification of procurement processes. Managing fewer suppliers reduces complexity, streamlines communication, and minimizes administrative overhead. This allows procurement teams to focus on strategic sourcing, supplier relationship management, and other value-added activities that can further enhance supply chain efficiency.

Furthermore, by carefully selecting and vetting suppliers, businesses can reduce the risk of supply chain disruptions due to supplier insolvency, quality issues, or other unforeseen events. Consolidating with financially stable and reliable suppliers can create a more resilient supply chain that can withstand unexpected challenges.

Navigating the Challenges of Consolidation

While vendor consolidation offers numerous benefits, it's essential to be mindful of potential challenges and take proactive steps to mitigate risks.

- **Supplier Dependency:** Relying on a single supplier can increase vulnerability to disruptions. If the supplier experiences production issues, financial difficulties, or other challenges, it can impact the entire supply chain. To mitigate this risk, it's crucial to maintain a backup supplier or diversify your supply base for critical items.

- **Supplier Selection:** Choosing the right suppliers is critical for successful vendor consolidation. It's essential to conduct a thorough evaluation of potential suppliers based on factors like cost, quality, reliability, innovation capabilities, financial stability, and cultural fit.

- **Transition Management:** The transition to a consolidated vendor base requires careful planning and communication to minimize disruptions. Ensure a smooth handover of responsibilities, establish clear communication channels, and maintain open dialogue with both existing and potential suppliers throughout the process.

Real-World Example: Streamlining Supplier Relationships in the Automotive Industry

A global automotive manufacturer, seeking to optimize its supply chain and reduce costs, embarked on a vendor consolidation initiative. They meticulously evaluated their existing suppliers based on various criteria, including cost, quality, delivery performance, and innovation capabilities. After a thorough analysis, they consolidated their supplier base for a critical component from five suppliers to just two.

This strategic move yielded significant benefits. The manufacturer was able to negotiate better pricing and terms due to increased purchasing volume. They also streamlined their procurement processes, reducing administrative overhead and freeing up resources for other strategic initiatives. The consolidation fostered closer collaboration with their key suppliers, leading to improved communication, joint problem-solving, and enhanced quality control.

Moreover, the reduced lead times and improved supply chain visibility resulting from the consolidation enabled the manufacturer to respond more quickly to changes in demand and minimize the risk of stockouts. This enhanced their overall competitiveness and contributed to their overall success.

Strategy 4: Identifying and Eliminating Inventory Cost Drivers

Inventory carrying costs can significantly impact profitability. To reduce these costs, it's crucial to identify and address the specific cost drivers within your supply chain.

Key Cost Drivers: Inventory carrying costs encompass a wide range of expenses, including:

- **Capital Costs:** The cost of financing inventory purchases. This includes interest payments on loans or lines of credit used to purchase inventory, as well as the opportunity cost of capital tied up in inventory instead of being invested elsewhere.

- **Storage Costs:** Warehouse rent, utilities, maintenance, security, and labor. These costs can be substantial, especially for businesses with large inventory volumes or those storing goods in prime locations. Optimizing warehouse space utilization, implementing efficient storage systems, and leveraging technology can help reduce these costs.

- **Obsolescence Costs:** The cost of inventory becoming outdated or unsellable due to technological advancements, changes in fashion, or other factors. This is particularly relevant in industries with rapid product lifecycles or where consumer preferences change frequently. Implementing effective demand forecasting, product lifecycle management, and inventory rotation strategies can help mitigate obsolescence costs.

- **Damage and Shrinkage Costs:** Losses due to damage, theft, or spoilage of inventory. These costs can be significant, especially for businesses dealing with fragile or perishable goods. Implementing robust security measures, proper handling procedures, and regular inventory audits can help minimize these costs.

- **Insurance Costs:** Premiums paid to insure inventory against loss or damage. The cost of insurance can vary depending on the type and value of the inventory, as well as the level of coverage desired. Businesses should regularly review their insurance policies to ensure they are adequately protected and explore options for reducing premiums through risk mitigation strategies.

- **Handling Costs:** Expenses related to moving, picking, and packing inventory. These costs can be significant, especially for businesses with high order volumes or complex fulfillment processes. Implementing efficient warehouse layouts, utilizing automation technologies, and optimizing picking and packing processes can help reduce handling costs.

- **Taxes:** Any applicable taxes on inventory held in stock. These taxes can vary depending on the location and type of inventory. Businesses should be aware of their tax obligations and explore opportunities for tax optimization, such as utilizing tax-advantaged inventory valuation methods.

Identifying and Addressing Cost Drivers: A Data-Driven Approach

Input Total Inventory Value on Hand (Monthly Basis)		$ 750,000.00

Inventory Holding Costs		Total
Cost of Money: Let's assume your yearly interest rate on loans and credit lines is 5%. This yearly interest rate can be transferred to a daily interest rate. Since you use money to purchase inventory, every day you hold inventory is a direct cost to your company.	5%	$ 37,500.00
Ruined Inventory: These are parts and materials that are damaged beyond repair. This is because of poor handling methods inside the warehouse. This happens frequently when inventory is not properly packaged and stored.	3%	$ 25,000.00
Electricity Costs: These are costs relating to lighting, and general electricity. It can also include the cost to keep the warehouse cool in the summer, and warm in the winter.	3%	$ 20,000.00
Lost Customers: It's common to lose customers because you did not have the inventory available, or the inventory you delivered was damaged. Very few companies track lost customers because of poor inventory management practices.	3%	$ 20,000.00
High Freight Costs: These costs occur when you have to pay expedited freight to rush parts and materials in because your inventory was low, or the inventory you did have, was damaged. This is also includes those times when you have to rush product to your customers because you didn't maintain a proper inventory count. *** Include an amount above and beyond your standard per-unit freight cost on incoming parts and raw materials.	7%	$ 50,000.00
Overtime: This is when your company pays overtime for employees to either receive, or ship out products. Again, this happens when you don't have the inventory available when it's needed and must therefore rush parts & materials into your warehouse.	3%	$ 20,000.00
Damaged Inventory: The more inventory is handled, the more likely damage will occur. This often happens when you have to move slow moving inventory to a new location in your warehouse to make room for faster selling products.	7%	$ 50,000.00
Dead Stock, Obsolete Inventory & Theft: These are parts that can not be sold because there is no use for them anymore. They can be considered obsolete or outdated products. In this case, they can only be sold for scrap. Included in this cost is the cost of theft.	7%	$ 50,000.00
Total Yearly Inventory Holding Costs	36%	$ 272,500.00

To optimize inventory costs, it's essential to adopt a data-driven approach that involves:

1. **Itemize Cost Drivers:** Create a detailed list of all inventory-related expenses, categorizing them into the various cost drivers mentioned above. This will help you gain a comprehensive understanding of your inventory cost structure.

2. **Calculate Monthly Costs:**
Determine the monthly cost of holding inventory, considering factors like storage space, insurance, obsolescence rates, and the opportunity cost of capital. This will provide a baseline for measuring your progress in reducing inventory costs.

3. **Isolate Areas of Concern:** Analyze the data to identify the cost drivers with the most significant impact on your bottom line. This will help you prioritize your cost-reduction efforts and focus on the areas where you can achieve the greatest savings.

4. **Implement Corrective Actions:**
Develop and implement strategies to address the identified cost drivers. This could involve reducing safety stock levels, improving demand forecasting, implementing lean inventory practices, optimizing warehouse space utilization, negotiating better payment terms with suppliers, or outsourcing warehousing or logistics functions.

5. **Measure Progress:** Regularly track and measure your progress in reducing inventory costs. This will help you evaluate the effectiveness of your strategies and make adjustments as needed. Utilize key performance indicators (KPIs) such as inventory turnover ratio, carrying costs as a percentage of inventory value, and stockout rates to monitor your progress and identify areas for further improvement.

Example: Streamlining Inventory Management at a Consumer Goods Company

A consumer goods company was facing escalating inventory carrying costs, impacting their profitability. They decided to conduct a thorough analysis of their inventory cost drivers using the steps outlined above.

Through this analysis, they discovered that a significant portion of their carrying costs was due to slow-moving and obsolete items, as well as inefficient warehouse operations. They also identified opportunities to improve demand forecasting and negotiate better payment terms with suppliers.

Armed with these insights, the company implemented a series of changes. They introduced a more sophisticated demand forecasting model, implemented a just-in-time inventory system for their fast-moving items, and liquidated their slow-moving and obsolete inventory through targeted promotions and online marketplaces. They also reorganized their warehouse layout, invested in new storage solutions, and implemented lean principles to optimize space utilization and reduce handling costs. Additionally, they negotiated extended payment terms with their key suppliers, improving their cash flow and reducing their reliance on external financing.

As a result of these efforts, the company was able to significantly reduce its inventory carrying costs, freeing up valuable capital and improving its overall profitability. They also saw improvements in customer satisfaction due to reduced stockouts and faster order fulfillment.

Strategy 5: Favorable Payment Terms and Improving Negotiation

Negotiating favorable payment terms with suppliers can significantly impact your cash flow and working capital. By extending payment terms or securing early payment discounts, businesses can delay cash outflows, improve their financial flexibility, and reduce their reliance on external financing.

Extended Payment Terms: Negotiate longer payment terms, such as net 45 or net 60 days, to delay cash outflows and improve your financial flexibility. This allows you to hold onto cash longer, potentially earning interest or investing it in other areas of the business.

Early Payment Discounts: Secure discounts or rebates for paying invoices early. This can lead to significant savings over time, especially for businesses with high invoice volumes.

Negotiation Skills: Empower your procurement team with strong negotiation skills. Effective negotiation can lead to better pricing, terms, and overall value from suppliers. Invest in negotiation training and development for your procurement team to ensure they have the skills and confidence to secure the best possible deals.

Collaborative Approach: Foster a collaborative approach to supplier negotiations, focusing on building long-term relationships based on trust and mutual benefit. This can lead to more favorable terms and greater flexibility in managing your supply chain.

Technology Solutions: Utilize procurement software and e-procurement platforms to streamline the negotiation process, track supplier performance, and identify opportunities for cost savings.

Conclusion: A Holistic Approach to Supply Chain Optimization

Effective supply chain management is not just about implementing individual cost-cutting strategies; it's about adopting a holistic approach that considers the interdependencies between various functions and processes. By aligning your supply chain strategy with your business needs, collaborating closely with suppliers, optimizing inventory levels, and leveraging technology, you can achieve significant cost savings, improve efficiency, and enhance customer satisfaction.

Remember, the pursuit of profit should not come at the expense of customer service or long-term sustainability. By striking the right balance between efficiency and responsiveness, businesses can create a supply chain that not only minimizes costs but also delivers value to customers and supports the company's overall growth and success.

Chapter 4: Five B2B Vendor Managed Inventory (VMI) Strategies: Pros & Cons for Vendors

Introduction: The Power of Partnership in Inventory Management

In today's intensely competitive business landscape, efficient inventory management has evolved beyond a mere logistical necessity into a strategic imperative. The ability to maintain optimal stock levels, reduce costs, and guarantee timely product availability can significantly impact a company's success. One innovative approach gaining traction is Vendor Managed Inventory (VMI), a collaborative model where the vendor takes charge of managing inventory levels at the customer's location. A recent study by ARC Advisory Group revealed that VMI can lead to a remarkable 20-30% reduction in inventory costs and a 10-15% improvement in customer service levels. These impressive figures underscore the transformative potential of VMI for both vendors and customers alike.

At its core, VMI is a partnership founded on trust and shared objectives. It represents a shift in responsibility, with the vendor assuming the crucial tasks of monitoring inventory levels, forecasting demand, and replenishing stock as needed. This collaborative approach paves the way for enhanced efficiency, cost reductions, and elevated customer satisfaction.

In this chapter, we'll delve into five distinct VMI strategies, each with its own unique advantages and challenges. By gaining a comprehensive understanding of these strategies, vendors can make well-informed decisions about which approach best aligns with their business model and customer relationships.

1. Vendor Onsite: The Embedded Partner

In this VMI model, a dedicated employee from the vendor is stationed at the customer's facility, taking ownership of managing the vendor's inventory on-site. This individual functions as an integral part of the vendor's team, working in close collaboration with the customer to ensure seamless inventory management. Their responsibilities encompass physically counting inventory, meticulously tracking usage, and strategically placing replenishment orders. They actively participate in the customer's inventory planning meetings, contributing valuable insights and recommendations based on their expertise. Their overarching goal is to prevent stockouts, minimize losses due to damage or theft, and continuously optimize inventory levels.

This model offers several distinct advantages. The vendor gains enhanced visibility and control, with direct access to real-time inventory data, allowing them to proactively address potential issues. Furthermore, the on-site presence fosters stronger customer relationships, cultivating closer collaboration and trust. This translates to improved service levels, as the vendor can swiftly respond to fluctuations in demand, ensuring product availability and minimizing the risk of stockouts.

However, the Vendor Onsite model does come with its challenges. Maintaining an on-site employee can be a considerable expense, particularly for smaller vendors or those serving multiple customer locations. Scalability can also be a concern, as this model may not be feasible for vendors with a vast customer base or geographically dispersed operations. Additionally, the on-site presence could potentially lead to conflicts or disagreements between the vendor's employee and the customer's staff, requiring careful management and communication.

Given these factors, the Vendor Onsite model is often best suited for high-volume contracts where the vendor supplies a substantial portion of the customer's inventory. It's also a valuable approach for scenarios where inventory management is complex, necessitating specialized knowledge or expertise. Moreover, companies prioritizing the cultivation of deep, collaborative partnerships with key customers may find this model particularly beneficial.

2. Replenishment Upon Visit: The Proactive Supplier

The Replenishment Upon Visit model is arguably the most prevalent VMI strategy, involving a vendor representative making regular visits to the customer's location to replenish inventory. This approach is commonly observed in retail environments, where vendors restock shelves with their products.

In this model, the vendor representative adheres to a pre-determined schedule, visiting the customer's location on a weekly or monthly basis. During these visits, they physically count inventory, assess usage patterns, and replenish stock to pre-agreed levels. The customer may also furnish the vendor with estimated usage data to facilitate planning and forecasting.

This approach boasts several advantages. It is generally more cost-effective than having a dedicated on-site employee, making it an attractive option for smaller vendors or those with limited resources. Moreover, its flexibility allows for adaptation across various industries and customer sizes. It also offers convenience to the customer, as the vendor assumes responsibility for inventory replenishment, freeing up the customer's time and resources.

However, the Replenishment Upon Visit model also presents certain challenges. The vendor's access to inventory data is limited to their scheduled visits, which could lead to delays in identifying and addressing issues. The accuracy of inventory replenishment hinges on the customer providing reliable usage data. Additionally, if demand fluctuates unexpectedly between visits, stockouts might occur.

Considering these factors, this model is well-suited for vendors servicing multiple customers within a defined geographic region. It's particularly effective for products with relatively stable demand patterns, where forecasting is more reliable. Smaller vendors seeking a cost-effective VMI solution may also find this approach appealing.

3. Vendor Access to Customer Inventory System: The Data-Driven Approach

In this technologically advanced VMI model, the vendor remotely manages the customer's inventory by accessing their inventory management system. This provides real-time visibility into stock levels and usage patterns.

The vendor is granted secure access to the customer's inventory system, such as their Material Requirements Planning (MRP) or Enterprise Resource Planning (ERP) system. They establish minimum and maximum inventory levels for their products and continuously monitor inventory levels. When stock dips below the minimum, the system automatically generates replenishment orders.

This data-driven approach offers several compelling advantages. The vendor enjoys real-time visibility into inventory levels, facilitating proactive replenishment and minimizing the risk of stockouts. Automation of replenishment processes reduces administrative overhead and minimizes errors. Additionally, access to historical sales data empowers the vendor to refine demand forecasting accuracy.

However, this model also comes with its share of challenges. Sharing sensitive inventory data necessitates robust security measures to safeguard both parties. Integrating the vendor's and customer's systems can be a complex and time-consuming undertaking. Furthermore, the customer may perceive a reduced level of control over inventory decisions compared to other VMI models.

Therefore, the Vendor Access to Customer Inventory System model is most suitable for tech-savvy companies where both the vendor and customer possess the technological infrastructure and capabilities to support seamless system integration. It's particularly effective for products with variable demand, as real-time data enables rapid adjustments to inventory levels. Moreover, companies with established trust and robust communication channels can leverage this collaborative approach to mutual benefit.

4. Barcode, Pictures, and/or Excel Sheets: The Hybrid Approach

This model represents a hybrid approach, blending elements of vendor-managed and consignment inventory, and heavily relies on collaboration and trust between the vendor and customer.

In this scenario, the customer diligently tracks inventory usage using various methods like barcodes, photos, or Excel sheets. They periodically share this data with the vendor, who then invoices the customer based on actual usage and replenishes inventory accordingly.

This hybrid approach offers simplicity, as it's relatively easy to implement without requiring extensive technology or system integration. It's also adaptable to different industries and product types, providing flexibility for vendors and customers. Additionally, it can be a cost-effective solution for smaller vendors or those with limited resources.

However, this model has its limitations. The accuracy of inventory data hinges entirely on the customer's diligence and accuracy in tracking usage. Data sharing and replenishment might not be as timely as in other VMI models, potentially leading to delays. Furthermore, the vendor has less visibility into real-time inventory levels compared to more integrated approaches.

Consequently, the Barcode, Pictures, and/or Excel Sheets model is often most appropriate for small-scale operations or businesses with relatively simple inventory management needs. It's particularly effective for products with stable demand patterns, where forecasting is less challenging. Moreover, this approach thrives in situations where a high level of trust exists between the vendor and customer.

5. Vendor Leases Warehouse Space: The Dedicated Facility

In this model, the vendor takes a more proactive approach by leasing warehouse space within or adjacent to the customer's facility. This affords them even greater control over inventory management and streamlines logistics operations.

The vendor maintains a dedicated warehouse space exclusively for their products. They manage inventory levels, replenishment, and order fulfillment directly from this location. This model can be further enhanced by combining it with other VMI strategies, such as on-site vendor representation or system integration.

The Dedicated Facility model offers several key advantages. The vendor gains maximum control over inventory management and logistics, enabling them to optimize processes and respond swiftly to customer demands. This streamlined approach can lead to improved efficiency and enhanced customer service levels. Furthermore, this model is inherently scalable, accommodating growing demand or expanding product lines.

However, it's important to acknowledge the challenges associated with this model. Leasing warehouse space can be a significant expense, especially in prime locations. Managing a dedicated warehouse also adds complexity to the vendor's operations. Moreover, if demand forecasting is inaccurate, the vendor might find themselves with excess inventory, leading to increased carrying costs.

Therefore, the Vendor Leases Warehouse Space model is typically more suitable for larger vendors with substantial inventory volumes. It's particularly beneficial for products with high or rapidly growing demand, where proximity to the customer is crucial. Companies seeking to deepen their collaboration and integration with key customers might also find this model strategically advantageous.

Pros and Cons of VMI: A Balanced Perspective

VMI presents a plethora of benefits for both vendors and customers, but it's crucial to weigh these advantages against potential drawbacks before embracing any VMI strategy.

Benefits of VMI	Drawbacks of VMI
•Secure position as incumbent Supplier •Reduce lost sales •Help customers plan inventory •Reduce per-unit freight costs	•Still have to cover carrying costs of inventory •Often expensive to manage •What happens upon cancellation?

On the plus side, VMI leads to improved inventory management, reducing the risk of stockouts and overstocks for both parties. This translates to enhanced customer service, fostering satisfaction and loyalty. Furthermore, VMI can generate cost savings for both vendors and customers through optimized inventory levels, reduced carrying costs, and streamlined logistics. The collaborative nature of VMI fosters stronger relationships, paving the way for long-term partnerships. Additionally, by ensuring product availability and visibility, VMI can drive increased sales for vendors.

However, VMI is not without its challenges. Implementing a VMI system may require investments in technology, personnel, and training. Sharing sensitive inventory data necessitates robust security measures to protect both parties. There's also the potential for conflicts arising from differing priorities or communication breakdowns. Customers might perceive a loss of control over their inventory management processes, while vendors could face risks associated with heavy reliance on a single customer.

Choosing the Right VMI Strategy: Key Considerations

Selecting the optimal VMI strategy for your business requires careful consideration of several factors:

- **Product Type and Demand:** The nature of your products, their demand patterns, and any seasonality factors play a crucial role in determining the most suitable VMI model. Products with stable demand might be well-suited for simpler models, while those with fluctuating demand might require more real-time visibility and responsiveness.

- **Customer Needs and Expectations:** Understanding your customers' inventory management practices and service level expectations is paramount. Some customers might prefer a hands-on approach with on-site vendor representation, while others might be comfortable with a more data-driven model.

- **Technological Capabilities:** Assess both your company's and your customers' technological infrastructure and readiness for system integration. More complex VMI models, such as those involving system integration, require robust IT capabilities.

- **Financial Resources:** Evaluate the costs and benefits of each VMI strategy in relation to your budget and resources. Some models, like leasing warehouse space, might involve higher upfront costs but could lead to greater long-term savings.

- **Relationship with Customers:** The level of trust and collaboration you have with your customers is a crucial factor. More collaborative models, like on-site representation or system integration, require strong partnerships built on trust and open communication.

Conclusion: A Strategic Approach to Inventory Management

Vendor Managed Inventory represents a paradigm shift in supply chain management, fostering collaboration, efficiency, and mutual benefit. By carefully selecting and implementing the right VMI strategy, you can optimize inventory levels, reduce costs, enhance customer service, and forge stronger relationships with your key partners. It's a strategic approach that can transform your supply chain into a source of competitive advantage, driving growth and profitability for your business.

As you embark on your VMI journey, remember these key takeaways:

- **Assess your needs and choose the right strategy:** Carefully evaluate your business requirements and select the VMI model that best aligns with your goals and capabilities.

- **Build strong partnerships:** Foster open communication and collaboration with your customers to ensure mutual success.

- **Invest in technology and training:** Equip your team with the necessary tools and knowledge to effectively manage VMI processes.

- **Monitor and adapt:** Continuously track performance metrics and adjust your VMI strategy as needed to respond to changing market conditions and customer demands.

By embracing VMI as a strategic initiative, you can unlock the hidden potential within your supply chain, driving efficiency, profitability, and customer satisfaction. It's a journey worth taking, one that can lead to sustainable growth and a stronger competitive position in the marketplace.

Chapter 5: Five Mistakes Business Owners Make That Kill Growth and Destroy Profit

Introduction: The Perils of Self-Sabotage

Imagine steering a ship through treacherous waters, navigating past hidden reefs and stormy seas. You've charted a course for success, but unbeknownst to you, there's a leak in the hull, slowly but surely taking on water. In the world of business, these leaks represent the common mistakes that entrepreneurs unwittingly make, hindering their growth and eroding their profits. While some errors are easily spotted and rectified, others lurk beneath the surface, insidiously undermining progress.

This chapter explores five such mistakes that can prove fatal to business growth. By recognizing these pitfalls and taking proactive measures to address them, entrepreneurs can steer their ventures towards a brighter and more prosperous future.

1. Relying Too Much on Outside Influences: The "One-Size-Fits-All" Fallacy

In today's information age, business owners are constantly bombarded with advice, strategies, and success stories. While seeking external perspectives is valuable, blindly adopting approaches without considering their relevance to your unique business can be disastrous.

It's not uncommon to see entrepreneurs captivated by a strategy that worked wonders for another company, only to implement it haphazardly and face disappointing results. The allure of a "proven" formula can be tempting, but it's essential to remember that every business operates in a unique context with its own set of challenges and opportunities.

For instance, a supply chain strategy that works flawlessly for a large multinational corporation might prove disastrous for a small, local business. Similarly, marketing tactics that resonate with one target audience might fall flat with another.

The key is to critically evaluate external advice and assess its applicability to your specific circumstances. Don't hesitate to seek guidance from mentors, consultants, or industry experts, but always filter their recommendations through the lens of your own business reality. Remember, there's no one-size-fits-all solution in the entrepreneurial world.

Illustrative Example: A small bakery, inspired by the success of a large online retailer, invested heavily in building an e-commerce platform and offering nationwide delivery. However, they failed to consider the perishable nature of their products and the high shipping costs involved. The venture proved unsustainable, draining their resources and diverting focus from their core local market.

The Solution: Contextualize and Adapt

- **Understand your business:** Conduct a thorough SWOT analysis (Strengths, Weaknesses, Opportunities, and Threats) to gain a deep understanding of your company's internal and external environment.

- **Define your target market:** Identify your ideal customers and their specific needs and preferences.

- **Evaluate external advice critically:** When considering advice or strategies from external sources, carefully assess their relevance to your business, market, and target audience.

- **Adapt and customize:** Don't be afraid to modify or tailor strategies to fit your unique circumstances.

- **Seek expert guidance:** If unsure, consult with experienced professionals who can provide tailored advice based on your specific situation.

2. Not Having an All-Encompassing Plan: The BHAG (Big Hairy Audacious Goal)

A ship without a destination is at the mercy of the winds and currents. Similarly, a business without a clear, ambitious goal lacks direction and purpose. The concept of a BHAG, popularized by Jim Collins and Jerry Porras in their book "Built to Last," emphasizes the importance of setting a bold, long-term goal that inspires and motivates the entire organization.

A BHAG is more than just a lofty aspiration; it's a strategic tool that fosters alignment, focus, and accountability. By establishing a BHAG and communicating it clearly to all stakeholders, business owners create a shared vision that guides decision-making and resource allocation.

Moreover, a BHAG serves as a constant reminder of the company's ultimate ambition, encouraging everyone to think big and push beyond their perceived limitations. It's a powerful motivator that can galvanize teams, attract top talent, and propel the business towards extraordinary achievements.

Illustrative Example: In the early 1960s, President John F. Kennedy set a BHAG for the United States: to land a man on the moon and return him safely to Earth before the end of the decade. This audacious goal galvanized the nation, sparked innovation, and led to one of humanity's greatest achievements.

The Solution: Set a BHAG and Create a Strategic Roadmap

- **Define your BHAG:** Articulate a clear, compelling, and ambitious long-term goal that inspires and challenges your organization.

- **Develop a strategic plan:** Create a roadmap outlining the key steps, milestones, and resources required to achieve your BHAG.

- **Communicate the vision:** Share your BHAG and strategic plan with all employees, ensuring everyone understands their role in achieving the goal.

- **Foster accountability:** Establish clear metrics and regularly track progress towards your BHAG.

- **Adapt and evolve:** Be prepared to adjust your plan as circumstances change, but remain committed to the overarching vision.

3. Penny Wise, Pound Foolish: Identifying and Addressing Cost Drivers

The adage "penny wise, pound foolish" aptly describes the tendency of some business owners to focus on short-term cost savings at the expense of long-term profitability. While cutting costs is essential, it's equally important to understand the true cost drivers within your business.

Many entrepreneurs obsess over easily identifiable "hard costs," such as material expenses or labor wages, while overlooking the often-hidden "soft costs" associated with inefficiencies, delays, or poor decision-making. This narrow focus can lead to missed opportunities for significant savings and improved performance.

For instance, a company might save money by purchasing cheaper raw materials, only to discover later that the lower quality leads to increased production defects, customer complaints, and ultimately, lost revenue. Similarly, neglecting employee training and development might seem like a cost-saving measure in the short term, but it can result in decreased productivity, higher turnover rates, and a damaged company culture in the long run.

The Solution: Adopt a Holistic Approach to Cost Management

- **Identify and track all costs:** Conduct a comprehensive cost analysis to identify both hard and soft costs within your business. Implement systems to track and monitor these costs regularly.

- **Prioritize cost drivers:** Focus on addressing the most significant cost drivers that have the greatest impact on your bottom line.

- **Embrace a long-term perspective:** Don't sacrifice long-term profitability for short-term gains. Invest in initiatives that may have upfront costs but yield significant returns over time.

- **Empower your employees:** Encourage employees to identify areas for cost reduction and process improvement. Recognize and reward their contributions.

4. Ignoring Marketing: "Your Value Assertion"

In the words of Peter Drucker, "The aim of marketing is to know and understand the customer so well the product or service fits him and sells itself." However, many business owners underestimate the power of marketing, viewing it as an unnecessary expense rather than a strategic investment.

Successful companies have a well-defined value proposition that clearly articulates the unique benefits they offer to their target market. They understand that marketing is not just about chasing customers for orders; it's about building relationships, establishing trust, and positioning your brand as the go-to solution for your customers' needs.

Ignoring marketing can lead to missed opportunities, stagnant growth, and a lack of brand awareness. In today's digital age, where consumers are constantly bombarded with information, a strong marketing strategy is essential for cutting through the noise and reaching your target audience.

Illustrative Example: A talented software developer created a groundbreaking application but struggled to attract customers. Despite the product's undeniable value, the lack of marketing efforts left it languishing in obscurity. After investing in a targeted marketing campaign, the developer saw a dramatic increase in downloads and user engagement.

The Solution: Embrace Marketing as a Strategic Asset

- **Define your value proposition:** Clearly articulate the unique benefits your product or service offers to your customers.

- **Understand your target market:** Identify your ideal customers and their specific needs and pain points.

- **Develop a comprehensive marketing strategy:** Create a plan that encompasses various channels, such as social media, content marketing, email marketing, and paid advertising.

- **Track and measure results:** Monitor the effectiveness of your marketing efforts and make adjustments as needed.

- **Build relationships:** Focus on building long-term relationships with your customers through consistent communication and engagement.

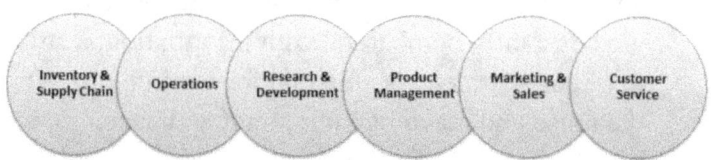

5. Setting Conflicting Goals and Objectives: "Defining Common Benchmarks"

While it's natural for different departments within a company to have their own goals and objectives, these goals should be aligned and complementary, not conflicting. When departments operate in silos with misaligned objectives, it can lead to inefficiencies, miscommunication, and ultimately, hindered growth.

For instance, if the sales team is solely focused on maximizing revenue, they might push for increased inventory levels to avoid stockouts. However, this could conflict with the procurement team's goal of minimizing inventory carrying costs. Similarly, the marketing team might prioritize brand awareness campaigns, while the finance team focuses on short-term cost-cutting measures.

The Solution: Foster Collaboration and Alignment

- **Establish common benchmarks:** Define overarching company goals and objectives that all departments contribute to. These benchmarks should be measurable and aligned with the company's overall strategy.

- **Break down silos:** Encourage cross-functional collaboration and communication to ensure that everyone is working towards the same goals.
- **Incentivize teamwork:** Implement performance metrics and reward systems that encourage collaboration and discourage competition between departments.
- **Regularly review and adjust:** Conduct periodic reviews to assess progress towards common benchmarks and make adjustments as needed.

Illustrative Example: A manufacturing company implemented a common benchmark of improving overall profitability. This goal united the sales, procurement, and operations teams, leading to improved collaboration and more efficient processes. The sales team focused on securing higher-margin orders, the procurement team negotiated better deals with suppliers, and the operations team streamlined production to reduce costs. As a result, the company achieved significant improvements in profitability.

Conclusion: Navigating the Path to Sustainable Growth

Running a successful business is a challenging endeavor, fraught with obstacles and pitfalls. However, many of these challenges can be overcome by avoiding common mistakes that hinder growth and erode profitability.

By recognizing the perils of relying too heavily on outside influences, setting ambitious goals, adopting a holistic approach to cost management, embracing marketing as a strategic asset, and fostering collaboration across departments, entrepreneurs can navigate the path to sustainable growth and long-term success.

Remember, the key to avoiding these mistakes lies in self-awareness, critical thinking, and a willingness to adapt and learn. By cultivating these qualities and proactively addressing potential pitfalls, you can steer your business towards a brighter and more prosperous future.

As you continue your entrepreneurial journey, keep these lessons in mind:

- **Contextualize and adapt external advice to your unique business.**

- **Set a BHAG and create a strategic roadmap to achieve it.**

- **Adopt a holistic approach to cost management, considering both hard and soft costs.**

- **Embrace marketing as a strategic asset to build brand awareness and drive customer acquisition.**

- **Foster collaboration and alignment across departments by setting common benchmarks.**

By avoiding these common mistakes and implementing these strategies, you'll be well on your way to building a thriving and sustainable business. The path to success may be challenging, but with the right mindset and approach, you can overcome any obstacle and achieve your entrepreneurial dreams.

Chapter 6: Calculating Economic Order Quantity (EOQ): The Science of Balancing Inventory Costs

Introduction: The High Cost of Inventory Mismanagement

In the fast-paced world of business, effective inventory management is more than just a logistical necessity; it's a strategic imperative that can significantly impact a company's bottom line. Picture a bustling warehouse, brimming with products ready to ship to eager customers. It's a sight that evokes a sense of abundance and success. However, this picture-perfect scenario can quickly turn into a costly nightmare if not managed carefully. Overstocked shelves, laden with slow-moving or obsolete items, tie up valuable capital and incur hefty storage costs, while empty shelves due to understocking lead to missed sales opportunities and frustrated customers.

The challenge lies in finding the elusive balance between having too much and too little inventory. This is where the concept of Economic Order

Quantity (EOQ) comes into play, offering a scientific approach to optimize inventory levels and minimize costs.

Understanding EOQ: The Quest for the Sweet Spot

Economic Order Quantity (EOQ) is the order quantity that minimizes the total cost of inventory management. It's the point where the cost of holding inventory (carrying costs) and the cost of ordering inventory (ordering costs) are in perfect harmony. By identifying and adhering to the EOQ, businesses can navigate the treacherous terrain of inventory mismanagement, ensuring they have just enough stock to meet demand without incurring undue financial burdens.

To truly appreciate the significance of EOQ, let's delve into the historical context of its development. The concept of EOQ emerged in the early 20th century, a time of rapid industrialization and growing complexity in supply chains. In 1913, Ford W. Harris, an American production engineer, developed the first economic order quantity model. However, it was R.H. Wilson, a consultant, who further refined the formula and popularized its use in 1934. The Wilson EOQ formula, as it's known today, has since become a cornerstone of inventory management, providing businesses with a powerful tool to optimize their inventory levels and minimize costs.

The Wilson EOQ Formula

$$\text{Economic Order Quantity} = \sqrt{\frac{(2 \times \text{Yearly Consumption}) \times (\text{Cost to Purchase})}{[(\text{Price}) \times (\text{Inventory Holding Cost} \%)]}}$$

The EOQ model is built on a simple yet profound principle: balance. It recognizes that there are two primary types of costs associated with inventory management:

1. **Ordering Costs:** These are the costs incurred every time an order is placed, regardless of the order size. They include administrative costs (such as processing purchase orders and communicating with suppliers), transportation costs, and receiving and inspection costs. Ordering costs tend to decrease as the order quantity increases, as fewer orders are needed to meet annual demand.

2. **Carrying Costs:** These are the costs associated with holding inventory in stock. They include storage costs (warehouse rent, utilities, etc.), capital costs (the opportunity cost of investing capital in inventory instead of other ventures), insurance costs, and the risk of obsolescence, damage, or theft. Carrying costs increase as the inventory level rises, as more space, capital, and resources are required to maintain the stock.

The EOQ model seeks to find the order quantity that minimizes the total of these two costs. It's like finding the perfect balance point on a seesaw, where the weight of ordering costs on one side is counterbalanced by the weight of carrying costs on the other.

The Wilson EOQ Formula: A Mathematical Expression of Balance

The Wilson EOQ formula elegantly captures this balance in a mathematical expression:

$$EOQ = \sqrt{(2DS)/H}$$

Where:

- EOQ = Economic Order Quantity

- D = Annual Demand (total units required per year)

- S = Ordering Cost (cost per order)

- H = Holding Cost (cost per unit per year)

This formula calculates the optimal order quantity that minimizes the total cost of inventory management by considering the trade-off between ordering costs and carrying costs.

Unveiling the Hidden Costs: Calculating the Components of EOQ

While the EOQ formula itself is straightforward, accurately calculating its components requires a meticulous examination of various cost elements. Let's delve deeper into each factor:

- **Annual Demand (D):** While most companies have a reasonable grasp of their annual demand based on historical sales data and forecasts, it's crucial to recognize that demand is rarely static. Seasonality, market trends, economic conditions, or even unforeseen events like natural disasters or pandemics can cause fluctuations. To ensure your inventory strategy remains effective, it's essential to incorporate demand forecasting techniques and maintain safety stock to buffer against unexpected changes.

- **Ordering Cost (S):** Determining the ordering cost requires a comprehensive analysis of all activities and expenses associated with placing and processing an order. It goes beyond the simple per-unit cost of goods. It includes:

  o **Administrative Costs:** Salaries of procurement staff, the time spent on creating and approving purchase requisitions, and communication with suppliers all contribute to the administrative overhead of placing an order. These costs can be significant, especially for businesses with complex procurement processes or a large number of suppliers. Streamlining procurement processes and leveraging technology can help reduce these costs.

  o **Transportation Costs:** The cost of shipping the goods from the supplier to your warehouse, including inbound freight charges and any other transportation-related expenses. These costs can vary depending on the distance, mode of transportation, and any special handling requirements for the goods. Negotiating favorable shipping terms with suppliers and optimizing transportation routes can help minimize these costs.

- Receiving and Inspection Costs: Once the goods arrive, there are costs associated with unloading, inspecting for quality and quantity, and storing them in the appropriate location within your warehouse. These costs can include labor, equipment, and any potential losses due to damaged or rejected goods. Implementing efficient receiving and inspection processes and investing in quality control measures can help reduce these costs.

- **Holding Cost (H):** The true cost of holding inventory often extends beyond the obvious expenses like warehouse rent, utilities, and labor. It's crucial to recognize the opportunity cost of capital tied up in inventory. This represents the potential return on investment if that capital were used elsewhere in the business rather than being tied up in unsold goods. This cost can be significant, especially for businesses with high-value inventory or limited access to capital.

Operation	Number of Tasks Completed	Hourly Rate	Total
Approvals	150	$ 40.00	$ 0.27
Purchase Requisition	150	$ 30.00	$ 0.20
Emailed Purchase Orders	150	$ 30.00	$ 0.20
Incoming Receipts	50	$ 20.00	$ 0.40
QC Inspection	75	$ 35.00	$ 0.47
Storage and Handling	75	$ 15.00	$ 0.20
Vendor Payment & Processing	130	$ 35.00	$ 0.27
		Cost to Purchase	$ 2.00

Other components of holding costs include:

- **Insurance Costs:** Premiums paid to insure inventory against loss or damage.

- **Taxes:** Any applicable taxes on inventory held in stock.

- **Obsolescence Costs:** The cost of inventory becoming outdated or unsellable due to technological advancements, changes in fashion, or other factors. Proper demand forecasting and inventory management practices can help mitigate this risk.

- **Damage and Shrinkage Costs:** Losses due to damage, theft, or spoilage of inventory. Implementing security measures, proper handling procedures, and regular inventory audits can help minimize these costs.

Accurately quantifying these costs demands a deep understanding of your business operations and a willingness to meticulously track and analyze various expense categories. Many modern

Enterprise Resource Planning (ERP) and Material Requirements Planning (MRP) systems can automate these calculations, providing more precise results than manual processes.

A Working Example: Illuminating the EOQ

Let's bring the EOQ calculation to life with a practical example. Consider a company with an annual demand of 5,000 units for a specific product. The ordering cost per order is $50, and the holding cost per unit per year is $2.

Applying the Wilson Formula, we get:

$$EOQ = \sqrt{(2 * 5000 * 50) / 2}$$

$$EOQ = \sqrt{500000}$$

$$EOQ \approx 707 \text{ units}$$

This indicates that the company should ideally order approximately 707 units per order to minimize its total inventory costs. By ordering this quantity, the company strikes a balance between the costs of placing frequent, small orders and the costs of holding large quantities of inventory.

A Working Example

The video above explains the following example in detail. However, to simplify the calculation, we'll review each step in detail.

- Annual or Yearly Consumption: 3000 units

- Price Paid Each Unit: $20.00

- Cost to Purchase: $2.00

The Wilson EOQ Formula

Economic Order Quantity: $\dfrac{\sqrt{(2 \times 3000 \text{ Units}) \times (\$2.00\,)}}{[(\$20.00) \times (3\,\%)]}$

Economic Order Quantity: $\dfrac{\sqrt{(6000 \text{ Units}) \times (\$2.00\,)}}{[(\$0.60]}$

Economic Order Quantity: $\dfrac{\sqrt{(\$12,000)}}{[(\$0.60]}$

Economic Order Quantity: $\sqrt{20,000}$

Economic Order Quantity: **141**

From the above example, the company's EOQ would be 141 units. Given that the company purchases 3000 units a year, it will then make 21 separate purchases of 141 units at a time. This is simply the 3000 units divided by the EOQ of 141.

Beyond the Formula: Navigating Real-World Complexities

While the Wilson EOQ formula provides a valuable framework for inventory management, it's important to recognize its inherent limitations. The formula operates under certain assumptions that may not always reflect the dynamic nature of the business world.

- **Constant Demand:** The formula assumes that demand remains constant throughout the year. In reality, demand can fluctuate due to seasonality, market trends, economic conditions, or even unforeseen events like natural disasters or pandemics. To ensure your inventory strategy remains effective, it's essential to incorporate demand forecasting techniques and maintain safety stock to buffer against unexpected changes.

- **Fixed Costs:** The formula also assumes that ordering and holding costs remain fixed. However, these costs can vary depending on factors like supplier relationships, transportation costs, and storage space availability. It's important to periodically review and update these cost estimates to ensure the accuracy of your EOQ calculations.

- **Instantaneous Replenishment:** The formula assumes that inventory is replenished instantaneously once an order is placed. In reality, lead times can vary due to production delays, transportation issues, or customs clearance. This variability can impact your ability to meet customer demand, necessitating adjustments to your reorder points and safety stock levels.

Adapting EOQ to Your Business

To ensure the EOQ model remains relevant and effective for your business, it's essential to adapt it to your specific circumstances.

- **Embrace Demand Forecasting:** If your business operates in a cyclical market with fluctuating demand, consider recalculating your EOQ periodically to reflect changing conditions. Leverage demand forecasting techniques, such as time series analysis or regression models, to anticipate future demand and adjust your order quantities accordingly. By proactively anticipating demand fluctuations, you can avoid stockouts and overstocks, ensuring that you have the right amount of inventory at the right time.

- **Factor in Quantity Discounts:** If your suppliers offer discounts for larger orders, it's essential to evaluate the potential cost savings against the increased holding costs. While bulk purchases can reduce the per-unit cost, they also lead to higher carrying costs due to increased storage and potential obsolescence. Conduct a break-even analysis to determine the optimal order quantity considering the discount structure. This will help you make informed decisions that maximize your overall cost savings.

- **Account for Lead Time Variability:** Supplier lead times can be unpredictable due to various factors like production delays, transportation disruptions, or customs clearance. This variability can impact your ability to meet customer demand, potentially leading to stockouts and lost sales. To mitigate this risk, consider building in buffer stock or safety stock to ensure you have enough inventory on hand to meet demand even if deliveries are delayed. You can use statistical methods to calculate safety stock levels based on your desired service level and lead time variability.

- **Leverage Technology:** Modern inventory management software and ERP systems can be invaluable in implementing and optimizing EOQ. These tools can help you track inventory levels, automate replenishment orders, generate real-time insights into your supply chain performance, and even incorporate demand forecasting and lead time variability into your EOQ calculations. By leveraging technology, you can streamline your inventory management processes, improve accuracy, and make data-driven decisions that enhance your overall efficiency.

- **Consider Other Inventory Models:** While the EOQ model provides a valuable framework, it's not the only approach to inventory management. Depending on your specific business needs and industry, other models like the Reorder Point (ROP) model or the Economic Production Quantity (EPQ) model might be more suitable. Explore different models and choose the one that best aligns with your unique circumstances.

- **Collaboration and Communication:** Effective inventory management requires collaboration and communication across various departments within your organization, including sales, procurement, operations, and finance. By fostering open communication and sharing data, you can ensure that everyone is on the same page and working towards the common goal of optimizing inventory levels and minimizing costs.

Conclusion: The Ongoing Pursuit of Inventory Optimization

Calculating the Economic Order Quantity is a crucial step towards optimizing inventory management and minimizing costs. However, it's not a one-size-fits-all solution or a magic bullet. It's a tool that requires understanding, adaptation, and continuous refinement to align with the ever-changing realities of the business world.

By diligently analyzing demand patterns, accurately calculating ordering and holding costs, and acknowledging the complexities of real-world supply chains, businesses can strike that elusive balance between having too much and too little inventory. This leads to improved operational efficiency, reduced costs, enhanced customer satisfaction, and ultimately, a healthier and more resilient business.

Remember, effective inventory management is not a one-time event but an ongoing process that demands constant vigilance, adaptability, and a willingness to embrace new technologies and approaches. By mastering the art and science of inventory optimization, you can transform your supply chain into a powerful engine for growth and profitability, ensuring your business thrives in today's dynamic marketplace.

Chapter 7: Five Costs of Low Inventory: How Being Too Lean Can Cost You

Introduction: The Hidden Dangers of the Lean Inventory Mindset

In the relentless pursuit of efficiency and cost reduction, the mantra of "lean inventory" has become a guiding principle for many businesses. The allure is undeniable: minimize inventory levels to free up capital, reduce storage costs, and avoid the risks associated with excess stock. However, this seemingly straightforward approach can be a double-edged sword. While lean inventory practices can yield significant benefits, there's a fine line between being lean and being *too* lean. When inventory levels dip below the optimal point, a cascade of hidden costs can emerge, threatening not only profitability but also the very survival of the business.

The Domino Effect of Stockouts: A Cautionary Tale

Imagine a bustling retail store on a busy weekend, teeming with eager shoppers ready to splurge. Yet, as they navigate the aisles, they're met with empty shelves and disappointed sighs. The desired products are nowhere to be found. Frustration mounts, and customers leave empty-handed, vowing to take their business elsewhere. Meanwhile, in a manufacturing plant, the rhythmic hum of production lines grinds to a halt as a critical component runs out of stock. The silence is deafening, as workers stand idle, deadlines loom, and the company incurs substantial losses in productivity and potential penalties.

These scenarios, while hypothetical, paint a vivid picture of the tangible and often painful consequences of low inventory levels. The impact isn't limited to the immediate loss of sales; it sets off a chain reaction that can reverberate throughout the entire organization. Customer relationships are strained, brand reputation suffers, and operational efficiency plummets.

The financial repercussions of stockouts are equally alarming. According to a study by IHL Group, stockouts cost retailers a staggering $634.1 billion annually in lost sales worldwide. This figure underscores the immense financial impact of inventory shortages. But the costs of low inventory extend far beyond missed sales opportunities. They can ripple through the entire organization, affecting customer relationships, operational efficiency, and overall profitability.

In this chapter, we'll embark on a journey to uncover the five key costs associated with low inventory levels, shedding light on the hidden dangers of being too lean. By understanding these costs and their potential impact, businesses can make more informed decisions about their inventory management strategies and strike the right balance between efficiency and customer satisfaction.

1. Lost Sales: The Immediate and Obvious Cost

The most immediate and obvious cost of low inventory is lost sales. When a customer is ready to buy but the product is out of stock, the sale is lost, along with the potential profit. This is a direct and quantifiable cost that can significantly impact a company's revenue.

To put this into perspective, let's consider a hypothetical scenario. A popular online retailer experiences a stockout of a highly sought-after gaming console during the holiday season. Each unit of the console sells for $500, and the retailer's profit margin is 20%. If they experience a stockout of 100 units, the immediate lost revenue is $50,000, and the lost profit is $10,000.

But the impact of lost sales goes beyond the immediate financial loss. It can also damage customer relationships and brand reputation. Customers who experience stockouts are more likely to switch to competitors, leading to a loss of market share and long-term revenue. In today's hyper-competitive marketplace, where customer loyalty is increasingly fragile, the ability to consistently fulfill orders and meet demand is crucial for sustainable growth. A single stockout can trigger a domino effect, leading to a decline in customer trust, negative online reviews, and a tarnished brand image.

To mitigate the risk of lost sales, businesses need to adopt a proactive and strategic approach to inventory management. This includes:

- **Accurate Demand Forecasting:** Utilize historical sales data, market trends, seasonality, and other relevant information to predict future demand and adjust inventory levels accordingly. Advanced forecasting techniques, such as machine learning algorithms, can help improve accuracy and anticipate fluctuations in demand.

- **Safety Stock:** Maintain a buffer stock to account for unexpected spikes in demand or supplier lead times. The level of safety stock should be carefully calculated based on historical data and risk tolerance.

- **Alternative Fulfillment Options:** Explore options like drop shipping or backordering to fulfill customer orders even when inventory is low. This can help maintain customer satisfaction and prevent lost sales.

- **Proactive Communication:** Keep customers informed about potential delays or stockouts, and offer alternative products or solutions whenever possible. Transparency and proactive communication can go a long way in mitigating the negative impact of stockouts on customer relationships.

By taking a proactive approach to inventory management and prioritizing customer satisfaction, businesses can minimize lost sales and protect their valuable market share.

2. High Freight Costs: The Price of Urgency

When faced with a stockout, businesses often resort to expedited shipping to replenish inventory quickly and fulfill customer orders. However, this urgency comes at a price. Expedited freight charges can be significantly higher than standard shipping rates, eroding profit margins and impacting the bottom line.

Imagine a manufacturing company that runs out of a critical component needed for production. To avoid costly downtime and delays, they opt for air freight to expedite the delivery of the component. While this ensures production can resume quickly, the air freight charges are substantially higher than the usual sea freight costs, cutting into the company's profit margins on the finished product.

In addition to the direct cost of expedited freight, there are other hidden costs associated with rush shipments. These can include:

- **Overtime Costs:** Receiving and inspecting expedited shipments often requires additional labor, leading to overtime costs for warehouse staff.

- **Supplier Surcharges:** Some suppliers may impose surcharges for rush orders, further increasing the cost of replenishment.

- **Production Delays:** If raw materials or components are out of stock, production may be delayed, leading to missed deadlines and potential penalties from customers or partners.

- **Administrative Overhead:** Managing expedited shipments often involves additional paperwork, communication, and coordination, adding to the administrative burden.

These costs can quickly accumulate, eating into profits and creating a financial strain on the business. To avoid these high freight costs, it's essential to maintain adequate inventory levels and implement efficient inventory management practices. This includes:

- **Accurate Demand Forecasting:** As mentioned earlier, accurate demand forecasting is crucial for avoiding stockouts and the need for expedited shipments. By anticipating demand fluctuations, businesses can plan their inventory levels accordingly and avoid last-minute rushes.

- **Supplier Collaboration:** Work closely with suppliers to establish reliable lead times and minimize the risk of delays. Building strong relationships with suppliers and establishing clear communication channels can help ensure timely deliveries and reduce the need for expedited shipments.

- **Inventory Optimization:** Implement inventory management techniques like ABC analysis to prioritize critical items and ensure adequate stock levels. This involves classifying inventory items based on their value and demand patterns, allowing businesses to focus their resources on the most important items.

- **Technology Solutions:** Utilize inventory management software and other technology solutions to track inventory levels, automate replenishment orders, and gain real-time visibility into your supply chain. These tools can help you identify potential stockouts early on and take proactive measures to avoid them.

By taking a proactive and strategic approach to inventory management, businesses can avoid the costly consequences of rush shipments and maintain a healthy bottom line.

3. Lost Profit: The Silent Killer

Every lost sale represents a lost opportunity for profit. In today's competitive landscape, where profit margins are often razor-thin, every dollar counts. Failing to make a sale due to a stockout can have a significant impact on a company's profitability.

To understand the true cost of lost profit, it's essential to consider the contribution margin of each product. The contribution margin is the difference between the selling price and the variable cost per unit. It represents the amount of money each sale contributes towards covering fixed costs and generating profit.

When a sale is lost due to a stockout, the company not only loses the potential revenue but also the contribution margin that would have gone towards covering fixed costs and generating profit. This can have a cascading effect on the business, potentially impacting marketing budgets, employee compensation, and investments in growth initiatives.

Let's illustrate this with an example. A furniture retailer experiences a stockout of a popular sofa model during a promotional sale. Each sofa sells for $1,000, and the contribution margin is 30%. If they miss out on selling 50 sofas due to the stockout, the lost revenue is $50,000, and the lost profit is $15,000. This lost profit could have been used to fund marketing campaigns, provide employee bonuses, or invest in new product development.

To mitigate the risk of lost profit, businesses need to focus on:

- **Optimizing Inventory Levels:** Maintain adequate inventory levels to ensure product availability and meet customer demand. This involves striking a balance between carrying costs and the risk of stockouts.

- **Improving Demand Forecasting:** Utilize advanced forecasting techniques, such as machine learning algorithms or predictive analytics, to predict future demand more accurately and avoid stockouts.

- **Pricing Strategies:** Implement pricing strategies that maximize profitability while remaining competitive. This involves understanding customer price sensitivity and adjusting prices based on demand and market conditions.

- **Cost Reduction:** Continuously look for ways to reduce costs throughout the supply chain, from procurement to production to logistics. This will help improve profit margins and make the business more resilient to fluctuations in demand.

By prioritizing profitability and taking a proactive approach to inventory management, businesses can avoid the silent killer of lost profit and ensure sustainable financial health.

4. Lost Customers and Market Share: The Long-Term Impact

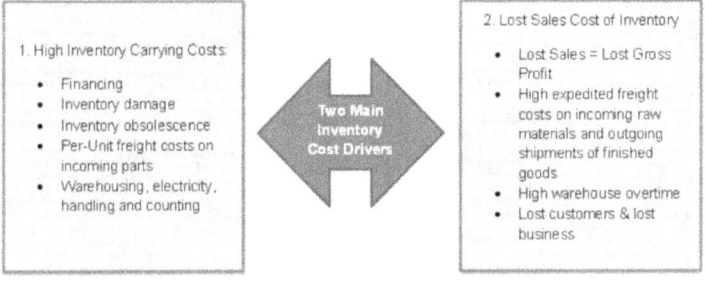

Losing a sale due to a stockout is not just a one-time loss; it can have long-term consequences for customer relationships and market share. Customers who experience stockouts are more likely to switch to competitors, leading to a loss of market share and a decline in long-term revenue.

In today's digital age, where information is readily available and customers have countless options, brand loyalty is more fragile than ever. A single negative experience, such as encountering an out-of-stock item, can trigger a customer to switch to a competitor, potentially never to return.

Once customers switch to competitors, it can be challenging and expensive to win them back. Competitors may solidify their position in the market, becoming the go-to supplier for your former customers. They may also gain a reputation for reliability and product availability, making it even harder for you to regain lost ground. Re-establishing trust and convincing customers to give you a second chance requires significant effort, time, and resources.

To prevent the erosion of customer loyalty and market share, businesses need to prioritize customer satisfaction and build strong relationships. This includes:

- **Proactive Communication:** Keep customers informed about potential delays or stockouts, and offer alternative products or solutions whenever possible. Transparency and proactive communication can go a long way in mitigating the negative impact of stockouts on customer relationships.

- **Exceptional Service:** Provide excellent customer service, going above and beyond to meet their needs and exceed their expectations. This includes offering personalized recommendations, resolving issues promptly, and providing a seamless shopping experience.

- **Loyalty Programs:** Implement loyalty programs or other incentives to reward repeat customers and foster long-term relationships. This can help create a sense of exclusivity and appreciation, encouraging customers to continue doing business with you.

- **Continuous Improvement:** Continuously seek feedback from customers and use it to improve your products, services, and overall customer experience. By actively listening to your customers and addressing their concerns, you can demonstrate your commitment to their satisfaction and build lasting relationships.

By prioritizing customer satisfaction and building strong relationships, businesses can mitigate the risk of losing customers and market share due to stockouts. Remember, acquiring new customers is often more expensive than retaining existing ones. Investing in customer loyalty and satisfaction is a wise strategy for long-term success.

5. Downtime: The Productivity Drain

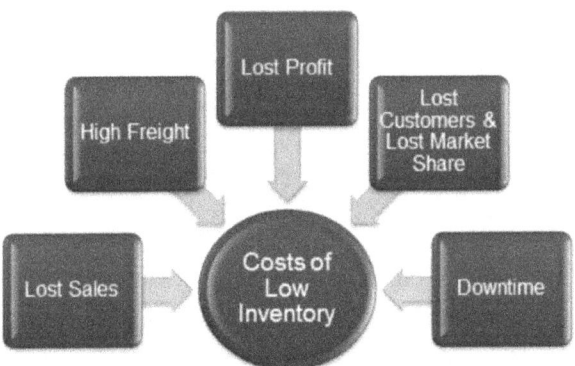

In manufacturing or production environments, low inventory levels can lead to downtime, where employees are idle and waiting for materials or components to arrive. This downtime can be incredibly costly, as it results in lost productivity, wasted labor hours, and missed deadlines.

Imagine a production line coming to a standstill because a key component is out of stock. Workers stand idle, machines lie dormant, and valuable time is wasted. The financial impact of this downtime can be substantial, as it directly affects the company's output and ability to meet customer demands.

But the cost of downtime extends beyond lost productivity. It can also have a negative impact on employee morale. Idle workers can become demotivated and disengaged, leading to decreased productivity even when production resumes. Additionally, downtime can disrupt workflows and create bottlenecks in other areas of the operation, further hindering efficiency.

If downtime leads to delays in fulfilling customer orders, it can damage customer relationships and lead to lost business. Customers expect timely deliveries, and any delays can erode their trust and confidence in your company.

To minimize downtime, businesses need to implement robust inventory management practices. This includes:

- **Accurate Demand Forecasting:** Anticipate future demand and ensure adequate inventory levels to support production schedules. Utilize historical data, market trends, and other relevant information to create accurate forecasts and avoid stockouts.

- **Supplier Collaboration:** Work closely with suppliers to establish reliable lead times and minimize the risk of delays. Communicate your production schedules and inventory needs clearly, and establish contingency plans in case of disruptions.

- **Safety Stock:** Maintain a buffer stock of critical components or raw materials to mitigate the impact of unexpected disruptions. The level of safety stock should be carefully calculated based on historical data, lead time variability, and risk tolerance.

- **Cross-Training:** Cross-train employees to perform multiple tasks, allowing them to shift to other areas of the operation during downtime. This can help maintain productivity and minimize the financial impact of disruptions.

- **Technology Solutions:** Implement inventory management software and other technology solutions to track inventory levels, automate replenishment orders, and gain real-time visibility into your supply chain. These tools can help you identify potential stockouts early on and take proactive measures to avoid them.

By prioritizing operational efficiency and taking proactive measures to avoid downtime, businesses can maximize productivity, reduce costs, and maintain customer satisfaction.

Conclusion: Striking the Perfect Balance

In the complex world of inventory management, finding the optimal balance between having too much and too little stock is an ongoing challenge. The Economic Order Quantity (EOQ) model provides a valuable framework for achieving this balance, but it's essential to recognize its limitations and adapt it to your specific business context.

By diligently analyzing demand patterns, accurately calculating ordering and holding costs, and acknowledging the complexities of real-world supply chains, businesses can strike that elusive balance between having too much and too little inventory. This leads to improved operational efficiency, reduced costs, enhanced customer satisfaction, and ultimately, a healthier and more resilient business.

Remember, effective inventory management is not a one-time event but an ongoing process that demands constant vigilance, adaptability, and a willingness to embrace new technologies and approaches. By mastering the art and science of inventory optimization, you can transform your supply chain into a powerful engine for growth and profitability, ensuring your business thrives in today's dynamic marketplace.

The five costs of low inventory—lost sales, high freight costs, lost profit, lost customers and market share, and downtime—serve as a stark reminder of the importance of maintaining adequate stock levels. By understanding these costs and implementing proactive inventory management strategies, businesses can avoid these pitfalls and achieve a sustainable balance between efficiency and customer satisfaction. The EOQ model, while not a perfect solution, provides a valuable framework for optimizing inventory levels and minimizing costs. By adapting the model to your specific business context, leveraging technology, and fostering collaboration across departments, you can achieve inventory equilibrium and position your business for long-term success.

In the end, effective inventory management is not just about numbers and formulas; it's about understanding your business, your customers, and your supply chain dynamics. It's about striking the perfect balance between efficiency and responsiveness, ensuring that you have the right products, in the right quantities, at the right time, to meet the ever-changing demands of the market and delight your customers.

Chapter 8: 10 Simple Solutions for Selling to Uncreditworthy Customers: Turning Credit Challenges into Opportunities

Introduction: The Untapped Potential of Uncreditworthy Customers

In the cutthroat world of sales, there's perhaps no greater frustration than watching a promising deal evaporate because the customer doesn't meet traditional credit standards. It's a scenario that can leave both the salesperson and the potential customer feeling disheartened and defeated. But what if we shifted our perspective and viewed these credit challenges not as roadblocks, but as gateways to untapped opportunities?

Consider this: a recent survey by the Small Business Administration revealed that nearly 40% of small businesses in the United States have been denied credit. This translates to millions of potential customers who are eager to do business but face obstacles in accessing traditional financing options. By developing strategies to cater to this underserved market, businesses can unlock a vast reservoir of untapped potential and gain a significant competitive edge.

Selling to uncreditworthy customers, however, is not without its complexities. It demands a nuanced understanding of credit risk, innovative financing solutions, and a willingness to adapt traditional sales practices. But the rewards can be substantial: increased sales, improved customer loyalty, and a more diversified and resilient customer base.

In this chapter, we'll embark on a journey to explore ten simple yet effective strategies for selling to uncreditworthy customers. We'll delve into the nuances of each strategy, providing real-world examples, actionable tips, and insights to help you navigate the complexities of credit risk and unlock new avenues for growth.

1. Staggered Invoice Dates: Easing the Burden of Prepayment

One practical solution for dealing with uncreditworthy customers is to stagger the purchase order and split the delivery dates on the invoice. This approach breaks down a large upfront payment into smaller, more manageable installments, making it easier for the customer to prepay.

For instance, instead of requiring a customer to prepay a $10,000 purchase order in full, you could divide it into five separate shipments of $2,000 each. Each shipment is released only after the customer has prepaid for that specific installment. This approach not only reduces the financial burden on the customer but also minimizes the vendor's risk of non-payment.

Advantages and Disadvantages

- **Advantages:** This strategy improves cash flow for the vendor, reduces the risk of non-payment, and makes the purchase more affordable for the customer, potentially leading to increased sales.

- **Disadvantages:** It can increase administrative overhead for the vendor due to the need to manage multiple invoices and shipments. There's also a risk of delays in order fulfillment if the customer fails to make timely payments.

- **Best Suited For:** Businesses selling high-value products or services, or those dealing with customers who have limited cash flow but are willing to commit to prepayment in installments.

2. Receivable Factoring: Sharing the Risk

Sometimes, the issue isn't the customer's creditworthiness but rather your company's own risk tolerance. Different companies have varying credit policies and risk appetites. What one company might consider a credit risk, another might view as an acceptable opportunity.

In such cases, receivable factoring can be a viable solution. This involves selling your accounts receivable to a third-party financing company, known as a factor. The factor will assess your customer's creditworthiness and may be willing to extend credit terms that your company wouldn't offer directly.

While factoring comes with fees, it can be a valuable tool for mitigating risk and improving cash flow, especially when dealing with uncreditworthy customers. It allows you to make sales that you might otherwise have to decline, opening up new opportunities for growth.

- **Advantages & Disadvantages:** Factoring provides immediate cash flow, reduces the risk of non-payment, and enables businesses to offer credit terms to customers they might otherwise decline. However, it can be expensive due to factoring fees, and the factor may have stricter credit requirements than the vendor.

- **Real-World Example:** A small manufacturing company secures a large order from a new customer with a less-than-stellar credit history. To mitigate the risk of non-payment, they opt for receivable factoring. The factoring company advances them a significant portion of the invoice value upfront, allowing the manufacturer to fulfill the order and maintain healthy cash flow.

- **Best Suited For:** Businesses with a high volume of accounts receivable or those looking to mitigate risk and improve cash flow, especially when dealing with new or unproven customers.

3. Credit Card Payments: Embracing Modern Payment Methods

The rise of e-commerce and digital payments has made credit card transactions increasingly common in the B2B space. While there are fees associated with accepting credit card payments, it offers a convenient and secure payment option for customers, including those with limited credit history or those who prefer not to use traditional credit terms.

By accepting credit card payments, you make it easier for uncreditworthy customers to do business with you. They can leverage their credit card limits to make purchases, and you receive payment upfront, eliminating the risk of non-payment.

- **Advantages & Disadvantages** Credit card payments offer convenience and security, providing immediate payment for the vendor and potentially increasing sales. However, processing fees can be high, and chargebacks can occur if the customer disputes the transaction.

- **Real-World Example:** An online retailer specializing in B2B sales implements a credit card payment gateway on their website. This allows them to attract a wider range of customers, including those who might not qualify for traditional credit terms. The convenience of credit card payments leads to increased sales and improved customer satisfaction.

- **Best Suited For:** Businesses selling products or services online, or those looking to offer a variety of payment options to their customers. It's particularly beneficial for businesses with a high volume of small-ticket transactions.

4. Smaller Credit Line & Partial Prepayment: Building Trust Gradually

For customers with recent or minor credit issues, offering a smaller credit line coupled with partial prepayment can be an effective strategy. This approach demonstrates goodwill and builds trust while mitigating risk for your company.

You can set the credit limit and prepayment percentage based on your assessment of the customer's creditworthiness and your own risk tolerance. For example, you might offer a $1,000 credit line with a requirement for a 50% prepayment on all orders. This allows the customer to make smaller purchases on credit while demonstrating their commitment to paying their invoices.

- **Advantages & Disadvantages:** This strategy helps build trust with new customers, reduces risk for the vendor, and can lead to increased sales over time as the customer's creditworthiness improves. However, it requires careful credit monitoring and may involve additional administrative overhead.

- **Real-World Example:** A wholesaler extends a small credit line to a new retailer with limited credit history. The retailer is required to make a 25% prepayment on all orders. As the retailer consistently makes timely payments, the wholesaler gradually increases their credit limit, fostering a mutually beneficial relationship.

- **Best Suited For:** Businesses willing to take calculated risks with new customers or those with minor credit blemishes. It's also suitable for businesses looking to establish long-term relationships with customers and gradually increase their credit limits as trust is built.

5. Bartering: Thinking Outside the Box

Bartering, the exchange of goods or services without the use of money, might seem like an ancient practice, but it can still be a viable option in certain situations, particularly when dealing with uncreditworthy customers. If a customer is unable to secure credit, consider exploring the possibility of bartering.

Think creatively about what your customer has to offer that could be valuable to your business. Perhaps they have excess inventory, equipment, or services that you could utilize. Or maybe they have connections or expertise in a particular market that could benefit your company.

While bartering requires careful negotiation and valuation of the goods or services being exchanged, it can be a win-win solution for both parties, enabling a transaction that wouldn't be possible through traditional credit terms.

- **Advantages & Disadvantages:** Bartering can facilitate transactions when credit is not an option, allows for creative solutions, and can lead to mutually beneficial partnerships. However, it can be complex to negotiate and value the exchange, and may not be suitable for all products or services.

- **Real-World Example:** A marketing agency offers its services to a local restaurant in exchange for meals for its employees. This arrangement benefits both businesses, allowing the restaurant to get professional marketing assistance without a cash outlay, and the agency to provide its employees with a valuable perk.

- **Best Suited For:** Businesses with flexible inventory or services, or those looking to establish relationships in new markets or industries. Bartering can also be a useful tool for businesses facing cash flow challenges or those operating in economies with limited access to credit.

6. Prepayment: Incentivizing Upfront Payment

In some cases, uncreditworthy customers may have no choice but to prepay for their orders. While this might seem like a limitation, it can actually be advantageous for your business. Prepayment eliminates the risk of non-payment and improves cash flow, allowing you to reinvest in your operations and fuel growth.

To encourage prepayment, consider offering a small discount or other incentives to customers who pay upfront. This can make the transaction more appealing to the customer and increase the likelihood of them choosing to do business with you.

- **Advantages & Disadvantages:** Prepayment eliminates credit risk, improves cash flow, and can be incentivized with discounts or other benefits. However, it may deter some customers who prefer credit terms, and could require additional administrative effort to process payments.

- **Real-World Example:** A software company offers a 5% discount to customers who prepay for their annual subscription

This incentivizes customers to pay upfront, improving the company's cash flow and reducing the risk of non-payment.

- **Best Suited For:** Businesses with low-risk tolerance or those selling high-value products or services. It's also suitable for businesses operating in industries with high credit risk or those dealing with customers in volatile markets.

7. Liquidating Outdated Inventory: A Mutually Beneficial Exchange

If you have slow-moving or outdated inventory taking up valuable warehouse space, consider offering it to uncreditworthy customers at a discounted price in exchange for prepayment. This benefits both parties: the customer gets a good deal on products they need, and you free up space and generate cash flow from otherwise stagnant inventory.

It's important to be transparent about the condition and age of the inventory, and to ensure that it still meets the customer's needs and quality standards. However, if done correctly, this strategy can be a win-win for both parties.

- **Advantages & Disadvantages:** This strategy helps clear out slow-moving or obsolete inventory, generates cash flow, and offers customers attractive discounts. However, it may require additional marketing and sales efforts, and could impact profit margins if discounts are too steep.

- **Real-World Example:** A fashion retailer offers a clearance sale on last season's apparel to uncreditworthy customers, requiring prepayment for all purchases. This allows them to clear out old inventory and attract new customers while minimizing credit risk.

- **Best Suited For:** Businesses with excess inventory or those looking to attract new customers with special offers. It's also a good option for businesses selling seasonal or perishable goods.

8. Warehousing: Leveraging Customer Assets

If you're struggling to penetrate a particular market due to high shipping costs or logistical challenges, consider partnering with an uncreditworthy customer in that market to utilize their warehouse space. This can provide you with a local presence and reduce your shipping costs, making your products more competitive.

In exchange for using their warehouse, you could offer the customer a discounted price on their orders or other benefits, such as priority access to new products or exclusive promotions. This creates a mutually beneficial arrangement where both parties gain from the partnership.

- **Advantages & Disadvantages:** This strategy reduces shipping costs, improves access to new markets, and strengthens customer relationships. However, it requires careful negotiation and coordination, and may involve additional logistical complexities.

- **Real-World Example:** A manufacturer of industrial equipment partners with a large customer in a remote location to use their warehouse space for storing and distributing products in that region. This allows the manufacturer to expand its reach without investing in a new warehouse, while the customer benefits from faster delivery times and potentially lower prices.

- **Best Suited For:** Businesses expanding into new markets or those facing high shipping costs. It's also a good option for businesses looking to build strategic partnerships with key customers.

9. Piggybacking on Your Customer's Freight: Sharing the Logistics Burden

If your customer has established logistics networks or expertise in shipping to specific markets, consider leveraging their capabilities to reduce your own freight costs and streamline your logistics operations. This can be particularly beneficial for businesses expanding into new markets or dealing with complex shipping requirements.

By partnering with your customer on logistics, you can tap into their knowledge and resources, potentially saving time and money. This collaborative approach can also strengthen your relationship with the customer and create opportunities for further collaboration.

- **Advantages & Disadvantages:** This strategy can lead to reduced freight costs, improved access to new markets, and streamlined logistics operations. However, it requires clear communication and coordination, and may involve sharing sensitive information with the customer.

- **Real-World Example:** A small exporter partners with a larger company that regularly ships goods to the same international market. By consolidating their shipments, they can both benefit from lower freight rates and simplified logistics.

- **Best Suited For:** Businesses with limited logistics expertise or those looking to expand into new markets with the help of established partners.

10. Receivables Insurance: Mitigating Risk

Receivables insurance provides coverage against non-payment by customers. While it comes with a cost and might be challenging to obtain for uncreditworthy customers, it can be a valuable tool for mitigating risk, especially when dealing with smaller or less established businesses.

The insurance will cover a predetermined percentage of your receivables, providing a safety net in case of non-payment. This can make it easier to extend credit to uncreditworthy customers, opening up new sales opportunities without jeopardizing your financial stability.

- **Advantages & Disadvantages:** Receivables insurance offers protection against bad debts and can facilitate sales to uncreditworthy customers. However, it comes with a cost and may require additional administrative effort.

- **Real-World Example:** A wholesaler selling to a network of small retailers purchases receivables insurance to protect against potential defaults. This allows them to extend credit terms to their customers, even those with less-than-perfect credit histories, without exposing themselves to excessive risk.

- **Best Suited For:** Businesses with a high volume of credit sales or those operating in industries with high credit risk. It's also a useful tool for businesses looking to expand their customer base and offer credit terms to a wider range of customers.

Conclusion: Embracing Flexibility and Creativity in Sales

Selling to uncreditworthy customers requires a shift in mindset and a willingness to explore alternative solutions. By embracing flexibility, creativity, and a collaborative approach, businesses can turn credit challenges into opportunities for growth and profitability.

Remember, every customer is unique, and there's no one-size-fits-all approach to addressing credit issues. Tailor your strategies to the specific needs and circumstances of each customer, and don't be afraid to think outside the box.

By implementing these ten strategies and fostering a collaborative approach with your customers, you can overcome credit hurdles, expand your customer base, and achieve sustainable growth. Remember, in the world of business, every challenge presents an opportunity. By embracing these opportunities and finding creative solutions, you can turn uncreditworthy customers into valuable partners and drive your business towards greater success.

Chapter 9: Advertising Isn't Marketing: It's Just One Piece of the Puzzle

Introduction: The Costly Misconception

Imagine a grand symphony orchestra, each musician playing their instrument with virtuosity. The strings create a lush tapestry of sound, the brass adds a triumphant fanfare, and the percussion provides a rhythmic heartbeat. But what if the conductor focused solely on the trumpets, neglecting the rest of the ensemble? The result would be a cacophony, a discordant mess that fails to capture the true beauty and power of the music.

In the world of business, this scenario mirrors the common misconception that advertising is synonymous with marketing. While advertising is undoubtedly a powerful instrument in the marketing orchestra, it's just one piece of the puzzle. Focusing solely on advertising, while neglecting other crucial aspects of marketing, can lead to a disjointed and ineffective strategy, much like a symphony dominated by a single instrument.

Consider the tale of a struggling restaurant owner who believed that a series of newspaper ads would magically revive their dwindling business. Despite their best efforts, the ads failed to attract new customers, leaving the owner perplexed and frustrated. The problem wasn't the quality of the ads; it was the lack of a comprehensive marketing strategy. The owner had focused solely on advertising, neglecting other critical elements such as market research, product development, pricing, and customer service.

This chapter aims to dispel the common misconception that advertising is the be-all and end-all of marketing. We'll explore the multifaceted nature of marketing, highlighting the crucial role of market expertise and strategic planning. By understanding the true essence of marketing and the strategic placement of advertising within it, businesses can unlock their full potential and achieve sustainable growth.

Defining Advertising and Marketing: Understanding the Difference

Before we delve deeper, let's establish clear definitions for advertising and marketing to avoid any further confusion.

- **Advertising:** Advertising is a paid form of communication designed to promote a product, service, or brand. It typically involves creating persuasive messages and delivering them through various channels, such as print, television, radio, online platforms, or outdoor displays. Advertising aims to capture attention, generate awareness, and ultimately drive sales.

- **Marketing:** Marketing is a much broader concept that encompasses all the activities involved in creating, communicating, delivering, and exchanging offerings that have value for customers. It's a strategic process that involves understanding customer needs and wants, developing products or services that meet those needs, setting appropriate prices, making the offerings available through the right channels, and promoting them effectively.

In essence, advertising is just one tool in the marketer's toolbox, a subset of the broader marketing strategy. While advertising can be a powerful tool for generating awareness and driving sales, it's most effective when integrated into a well-defined marketing plan that aligns with the company's overall goals and objectives.

The Importance of Market Expertise: Knowledge is Power

Successful marketing is built on a foundation of market expertise. To truly connect with your target audience and achieve your business goals, you need to have a deep understanding of your market, your customers, and your competitors.

This involves:

- **Understanding Your Customers:** Who are your ideal customers? What are their needs, pain points, and motivations? How do they make purchasing decisions? What channels do they use to gather information and interact with brands? Understanding your customers on a granular level allows you to tailor your marketing messages and offerings to resonate with them.

- **Analyzing Your Competitors:** Who are your main competitors? What are their strengths and weaknesses? How do they position their products or services in the market? What marketing strategies are they using? By analyzing your competitors, you can identify opportunities to differentiate your brand and gain a competitive advantage.

- **Identifying Market Trends:** What are the current trends and developments in your industry? How are customer preferences and behaviors evolving? What new technologies or innovations are disrupting the market? Staying abreast of market trends allows you to anticipate changes and adapt your marketing strategies accordingly.

By investing time and resources in market research and analysis, businesses can gain valuable insights that inform their marketing strategies and enable them to make informed decisions. This knowledge is power, allowing you to create targeted campaigns, develop compelling messages, and allocate resources effectively.

The Components of a Marketing Strategy: A Holistic Approach

A comprehensive marketing strategy encompasses various elements that work together to achieve the company's goals. While advertising plays a crucial role, it's just one piece of the puzzle. Other key components include:

- **Market Research:** This involves gathering and analyzing information about the market, customers, and competitors to inform marketing decisions. It's the foundation upon which a successful marketing strategy is built.

- **Product Development:** Creating products or services that meet the needs and desires of the target market. This involves understanding customer pain points, identifying opportunities for innovation, and developing offerings that provide value and solve problems.

- **Pricing:** Setting prices that reflect the value of the offering and align with the company's profitability goals. Pricing strategy involves considering factors such as production costs, competitor pricing, and customer perceived value.

- **Distribution:** Making the product or service available to customers through the most effective channels. This could involve direct sales, online platforms, retail partnerships, or a combination of channels.

- **Promotion:** Communicating the value of the offering to the target market through various channels, including advertising, public relations, sales promotions, and personal selling. Promotion aims to create awareness, generate interest, and ultimately drive sales.

- **Customer Relationship Management:** Building and maintaining strong relationships with customers to foster loyalty and repeat business. This involves providing excellent customer service, personalized communication, and ongoing engagement to create a positive customer experience.

Each of these components plays a vital role in the overall marketing strategy, and they must be carefully coordinated to achieve maximum impact. A successful marketing strategy is not just about executing individual tactics; it's about creating a cohesive and integrated approach that delivers a consistent message and experience to the customer.

The Role of Advertising: Amplifying Your Message

Advertising is a powerful tool for reaching a large audience and generating awareness for your brand, products, or services. It can be used to:

- **Create Brand Awareness:** Introduce your brand to the market and build recognition through memorable slogans, visuals, and storytelling.

- **Generate Leads:** Attract potential customers and encourage them to take action, such as visiting your website, signing up for a newsletter, or requesting a quote.

- **Promote Sales and Special Offers:** Drive sales by highlighting promotions, discounts, or limited-time offers. Create a sense of urgency and excitement to motivate customers to take action.

- **Reinforce Brand Image:** Communicate your brand values and personality to create a positive impression and foster emotional connections with your audience.

- **Support Other Marketing Efforts:** Complement other marketing activities, such as public relations or content marketing, to create a cohesive and impactful message. Advertising can be used to drive traffic to your website or social media pages, where you can further engage with potential customers and nurture leads.

However, for advertising to be effective, it must be strategically aligned with your overall marketing goals and target audience. It's essential to:

- **Define Your Target Audience:** Clearly identify the specific group of people you want to reach with your advertising. This involves understanding their demographics, interests, behaviors, and pain points.

- **Craft Compelling Messages:** Develop clear, concise, and persuasive messages that resonate with your target audience and highlight the benefits of your offering. Use strong visuals and storytelling to capture attention and create an emotional connection.

- **Choose the Right Channels:** Select the most appropriate advertising channels to reach your target audience effectively. This could include traditional media like print or television, or digital channels like social media, search engine advertising, or display advertising. Consider the cost, reach, and engagement potential of each channel.

- **Track and Measure Results:** Monitor the performance of your advertising campaigns using key performance indicators (KPIs) such as impressions, clicks, conversions, and return on ad spend (ROAS). Use this data to optimize your campaigns and allocate your budget effectively.

Conclusion: The Power of a Holistic Marketing Approach

In conclusion, while advertising is an important component of marketing, it's not the only one. To achieve sustainable growth and success, businesses need to adopt a holistic marketing approach that encompasses market research, product development, pricing, distribution, promotion, and customer relationship management.

By becoming a market expert, understanding your customers, and developing a comprehensive marketing strategy, you can leverage advertising effectively to amplify your message, reach your target audience, and achieve your business goals. Remember, advertising is just one piece of the puzzle. By focusing on the big picture and integrating advertising into a well-rounded marketing plan, you can unlock the full potential of your business and achieve lasting success.

In the words of the legendary marketer Philip Kotler, "Marketing is not the art of finding clever ways to dispose of what you make. It is the art of creating genuine customer value." By embracing this philosophy and adopting a holistic marketing approach, you can build a brand that resonates with your audience, fosters loyalty, and drives sustainable growth.

Chapter 10: The Pareto Principle in Business: Unlocking the Power of the Vital Few

Introduction: Unveiling the 80/20 Rule

In the intricate tapestry of business operations, where countless factors intertwine to influence outcomes, a simple yet profound principle emerges: the Pareto Principle, often referred to as the 80/20 rule. This principle, first observed by Italian economist Vilfredo Pareto in 1906, states that roughly 80% of effects come from 20% of causes. In essence, a small fraction of inputs or efforts often generates a disproportionately large share of the results.

Pareto's initial observation stemmed from his study of land ownership in Italy, where he noticed that 80% of the land was owned by 20% of the population. However, he soon realized that this pattern of imbalance extended far beyond land ownership. He found similar distributions in various other aspects of society and the economy, leading him to formulate the now-famous 80/20 rule.

The Pareto Principle's applicability has since been recognized in a wide array of fields, from science and engineering to social sciences and even personal development. In business, it has proven to be a remarkably versatile concept, revealing hidden patterns and imbalances in areas such as sales, marketing, manufacturing, operations, and inventory management. By understanding and leveraging this principle, businesses can identify the "vital few" factors that drive the majority of their results, allowing them to focus their efforts on what truly matters and achieve greater efficiency and effectiveness.

The Pareto Principle in Sales and Revenue: Nurturing Key Accounts and Expanding Horizons

In the realm of sales, the Pareto Principle often manifests as the 80/20 rule of customer revenue. This means that a significant portion, typically around 80%, of a company's sales revenue is generated by a relatively small percentage, around 20%, of its customers. These high-value customers, often referred to as "key accounts," play a crucial role in a company's financial success.

Recognizing and nurturing these key accounts is essential for any business. This might involve assigning dedicated account managers, providing personalized service and support, offering exclusive discounts or promotions, and proactively seeking feedback to ensure their needs are met. Building strong relationships with key accounts can lead to increased customer loyalty, repeat business, and positive word-of-mouth referrals.

However, while focusing on key accounts is important, it's equally crucial to avoid becoming overly reliant on a small group of customers. Over-reliance on a few large clients can create vulnerabilities. What if one or more of these major customers were to suddenly leave? The impact on revenue could be devastating, especially if the company hasn't cultivated relationships with other customers in the market. The 2008 global financial crisis served as a stark reminder of this risk, as many businesses that had heavily depended on a few large clients found themselves struggling to survive when those clients faced financial difficulties.

Therefore, it's essential to strike a balance between nurturing key accounts and expanding your customer base. By actively seeking new business opportunities and diversifying your revenue streams, you can mitigate the risk of over-reliance and ensure the long-term sustainability of your business. This might involve investing in marketing and sales efforts to attract new customers, exploring new markets or product lines, or developing strategic partnerships to expand your reach.

The Pareto Principle can also be applied within individual sales territories or geographic regions. By analyzing sales data and identifying the areas that generate the most revenue, businesses can allocate their sales resources more effectively. This might involve focusing on high-potential markets, assigning more experienced salespeople to key territories, or tailoring sales strategies to specific customer segments within each region.

The Pareto Principle in Marketing: Maximizing ROI with Targeted Efforts

In the dynamic world of marketing, where countless channels and tactics compete for attention, the Pareto Principle can serve as a guiding light. It often manifests as the 80/20 rule of lead generation, suggesting that 80% of your leads are likely generated by the top 20% of your marketing initiatives.

For businesses striving to optimize their marketing efforts and maximize return on investment (ROI), identifying these high-performing initiatives is crucial. This involves analyzing data from various marketing channels, such as social media, email marketing, content marketing, and paid advertising, to pinpoint the channels and tactics that yield the highest returns in terms of leads, conversions, and customer acquisition.

Once these "vital few" marketing initiatives are identified, businesses can focus their resources and efforts on these areas, maximizing their impact and minimizing wasted spending. This might involve reallocating budgets from underperforming channels to those that consistently deliver results, refining messaging and targeting to improve conversion rates, or investing in new technologies and tools to enhance marketing effectiveness.

Moreover, the Pareto Principle encourages marketers to think beyond traditional metrics like impressions or clicks and focus on the actions that truly matter, such as leads generated, sales closed, and customer lifetime value. By prioritizing these high-impact activities and tracking their performance, businesses can gain a deeper understanding of what works and what doesn't, allowing them to make data-driven decisions and continuously improve their marketing strategies.

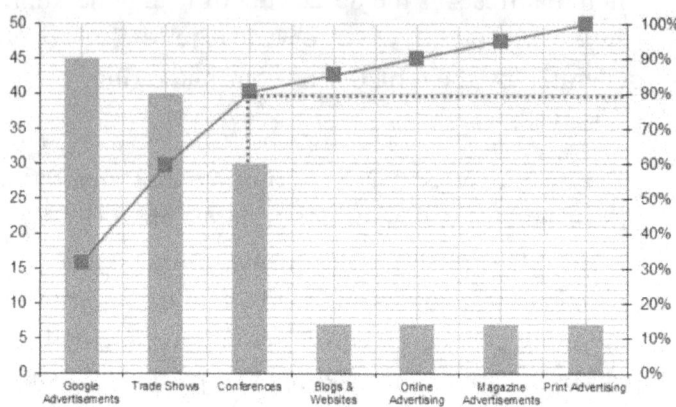

The Pareto Principle in Manufacturing: Streamlining Operations and Boosting Productivity

In the realm of manufacturing, the Pareto Principle can be a powerful tool for identifying the root causes of downtime and production bottlenecks. The 80/20 rule suggests that 80% of downtime is often caused by just 20% of the possible factors. This insight can help manufacturers focus their improvement efforts on the most critical areas, leading to significant gains in productivity and efficiency.

For instance, a manufacturing plant might experience frequent downtime due to equipment malfunctions, material shortages, or operator errors. By conducting a thorough analysis of downtime data and applying the Pareto Principle, they might discover that a small number of machines or processes are responsible for the majority of disruptions. This allows them to prioritize maintenance and improvement efforts, targeting the root causes of downtime and minimizing its impact on production.

Lean manufacturing, Six Sigma, and other continuous improvement methodologies often leverage the Pareto Principle to identify and prioritize areas for improvement. By focusing on the "vital few" causes that have the greatest impact on performance, businesses can achieve significant gains with minimal effort. This approach can lead to reduced waste, improved quality, increased throughput, and ultimately, a more competitive and profitable operation.

Causes of Lost Time	Incidences of Lost Time	Individual Percentages	Total Percentages
work instructions	45	31%	31%
bill of materials "BOM"	40	28%	59%
work orders	30	21%	80%
OOS: out-of-stock	7	5%	85%
wrong parts or material	7	5%	90%
lack of proper tools	7	5%	95%
bad assembly outlines	7	5%	100%
Total	143		

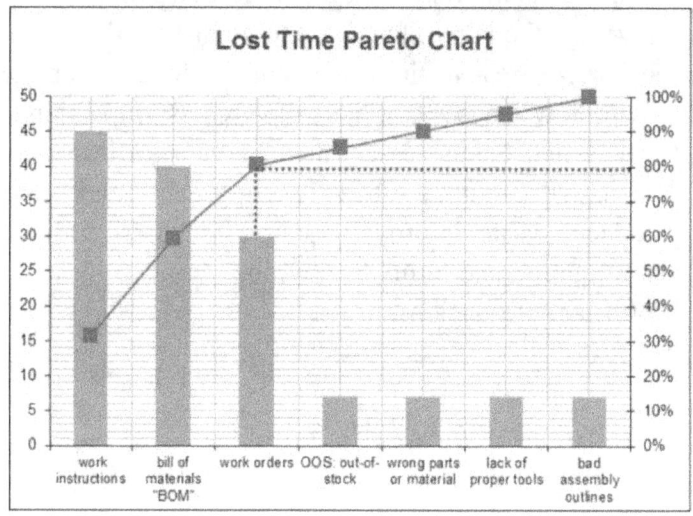

The Pareto Principle in Operations: Recognizing High-Performers and Addressing Inefficiencies

While the application of the Pareto Principle in operations might not be as clear-cut as in other areas, it can still offer valuable insights. The general idea is that 80% of the work is often done by 20% of the employees. This observation highlights the importance of recognizing and rewarding high-performing individuals who consistently contribute to the company's success.

However, the Pareto Principle in operations also underscores the need to identify areas where productivity might be lagging and take steps to address those issues. This might involve analyzing performance data, conducting employee surveys, or observing workflows to pinpoint areas for improvement. By addressing these inefficiencies through training, coaching, or process redesign, businesses can boost overall productivity and create a more engaged and motivated workforce.

It's important to note that the 80/20 distribution in operations might not always be precise. However, the underlying principle remains valid: a small percentage of factors or individuals often have a disproportionate impact on overall performance. By identifying and leveraging these "vital few," businesses can achieve significant improvements in efficiency and effectiveness.

The Pareto Principle in Inventory & Supply Chain Management: Optimizing Stock Levels

In the realm of inventory and supply chain management, the Pareto Principle can be a valuable tool for optimizing stock levels and reducing carrying costs. The 80/20 rule suggests that 80% of your sales likely come from the top 20% of your product line. This insight can help businesses identify their most profitable products and focus their inventory management efforts accordingly.

By analyzing sales data and applying the Pareto Principle, businesses can identify slow-moving or obsolete items that are tying up valuable capital and incurring unnecessary holding costs. These items can then be strategically liquidated through discounts or promotions, freeing up warehouse space and improving cash flow.

Furthermore, the Pareto Principle can guide businesses in prioritizing their inventory replenishment efforts. By focusing on the top 20% of products that generate the most sales, businesses can ensure that these items are always in stock, minimizing the risk of stockouts and lost sales opportunities. This approach allows businesses to allocate their resources more efficiently and avoid overstocking less popular items.

In addition to identifying key products, the Pareto Principle can also be applied to other aspects of inventory and supply chain management, such as:

- **Supplier Management:** Identify the 20% of suppliers that account for 80% of your purchases and focus on building stronger relationships with them.

- **Warehouse Optimization:** Analyze inventory turnover rates to identify the 20% of items that occupy 80% of your warehouse space and optimize their storage locations.

- **Transportation Management:** Identify the 20% of shipping routes or carriers that account for 80% of your transportation costs and explore opportunities for consolidation or negotiation.

Conclusion: The Pareto Principle as a Guiding Light

The Pareto Principle is a powerful tool that can be applied across various aspects of business operations. By recognizing the inherent imbalances and focusing on the "vital few" that drive the majority of results, businesses can optimize their efforts, increase efficiency, and achieve sustainable growth.

From sales and marketing to manufacturing, operations, and inventory management, the Pareto Principle offers a valuable lens through which to view and analyze your business. It encourages you to identify the key drivers of success and focus your resources on those areas that truly matter. By doing so, you can achieve greater efficiency, profitability, and overall business excellence.

The Pareto Principle in Action: Real-World Examples

To further illustrate the power of the Pareto Principle, let's explore some real-world examples of how businesses have leveraged this concept to achieve remarkable results:

- **Sales:** A software company discovered that 80% of its revenue came from 20% of its clients. By focusing on providing exceptional service and support to these key accounts, they were able to increase customer retention and drive even more revenue growth.

- **Marketing:** An e-commerce retailer analyzed their marketing data and found that 80% of their sales came from 20% of their email subscribers. They then tailored their email marketing campaigns to focus on these high-value subscribers, resulting in increased open rates, click-through rates, and conversions.

- **Manufacturing:** A manufacturing plant implemented a Pareto analysis to identify the root causes of downtime. They discovered that 80% of their downtime was caused by just three types of equipment malfunctions. By focusing on improving the maintenance and reliability of these machines, they were able to significantly reduce downtime and increase production output.

- **Operations:** A service-based company analyzed their employee performance data and found that 20% of their employees were responsible for 80% of the completed tasks. They then implemented a recognition and reward program to acknowledge and incentivize these high-performing individuals, leading to increased motivation and productivity across the entire team.

- **Inventory Management:** A wholesaler applied the Pareto Principle to their inventory and discovered that 80% of their sales came from 20% of their product lines. They then focused on optimizing the inventory levels for these high-selling products, reducing carrying costs and improving overall profitability.

Going Beyond the 80/20: The Pareto Chart

While the 80/20 distribution is a common manifestation of the Pareto Principle, it's not always a perfect fit. In some cases, the distribution might be 70/30, 90/10, or even more skewed. To gain a more precise understanding of the underlying patterns in your business, you can use a visual tool called a Pareto chart.

A Pareto chart is a bar graph where the bars are arranged in descending order of frequency or impact. This allows you to quickly visualize the relative importance of different factors and identify the "vital few" that contribute the most to a particular outcome. By using Pareto charts, you can make more informed decisions about where to focus your efforts and resources.

Limitations of the Pareto Principle

While the Pareto Principle is a powerful tool, it's important to recognize its limitations. It's not a universal law that applies to every situation. In some cases, the distribution might be more balanced, or other factors might play a more significant role in determining outcomes.

Furthermore, the Pareto Principle should not be used as an excuse to neglect the "trivial many." While focusing on the "vital few" is important, it's also essential to maintain a certain level of attention and effort towards the remaining factors. Neglecting these factors completely could lead to unforeseen consequences and missed opportunities.

Conclusion: The Pareto Principle as a Guiding Light

The Pareto Principle is a valuable concept that can help businesses gain deeper insights into their operations and make more informed decisions. By recognizing the inherent imbalances and focusing on the "vital few" that drive the majority of results, businesses can optimize their efforts, increase efficiency, and achieve sustainable growth.

However, it's important to remember that the Pareto Principle is just one tool in your toolbox. It should be used in conjunction with other analytical and decision-making frameworks to ensure a holistic and balanced approach to business management.

By embracing the Pareto Principle and using it judiciously, you can unlock the hidden potential within your business, identify areas for improvement, and make strategic choices that lead to greater efficiency, profitability, and overall success. Remember, it's not about working harder; it's about working smarter, focusing your efforts where they will have the greatest impact, and leveraging the power of the vital few to achieve extraordinary results.

Chapter 11: JIT Safety Stock: Even Just in Time Needs Just In Case Inventory

Introduction: The Unforeseen Turbulence in the Lean Supply Chain

The allure of Just-in-Time (JIT) inventory management, with its promise of minimal inventory, reduced carrying costs, and streamlined operations, has captivated businesses across industries for decades. It's a philosophy that seeks to eliminate waste by producing or procuring goods only as needed, thereby minimizing the costs and risks associated with excess inventory. However, the relentless pursuit of leanness can sometimes lead to a precarious situation, where the slightest disruption in the supply chain can trigger a domino effect of delays, shortages, and lost revenue.

The image of a perfectly synchronized assembly line, where each component arrives just in time to be fitted into the next product, is a testament to the power of JIT. Yet, this idealized vision often clashes with the realities of a complex and unpredictable world. What happens when a sudden labor strike at a key supplier disrupts the flow of raw materials? Or when a natural disaster throws transportation networks into disarray, causing delays in deliveries? The once-smooth operation grinds to a halt, workers stand idle, and the company incurs significant losses in productivity and revenue.

These scenarios underscore a crucial reality: even the most meticulously planned JIT systems are vulnerable to unforeseen events. That's where safety stock enters the picture, acting as a buffer, a safety net that protects against the inherent uncertainties of the supply chain. Despite the common misconception that JIT eliminates the need for safety stock, the truth is that even the leanest operations require a certain level of "just in case" inventory to ensure resilience and responsiveness in the face of disruptions.

The Misconception of JIT and Safety Stock: Dispelling the Myth

The Just-in-Time philosophy, pioneered by Toyota in the 1970s, revolutionized manufacturing and supply chain management. Its core principle is to eliminate waste, and excess inventory is considered a prime example of waste. The ideal JIT system, with perfect demand forecasting and flawless supplier reliability, would theoretically operate without any buffer inventory.

However, this idealized vision rarely translates seamlessly into the real world. Supply chains are complex and dynamic, subject to various uncertainties and disruptions. Customer demand can fluctuate unexpectedly due to changes in market trends, economic conditions, or unforeseen events. Suppliers can experience delays due to production issues, transportation disruptions, or natural disasters. Even the most reliable suppliers can encounter unforeseen challenges that impact their ability to deliver on time.

In such situations, safety stock acts as a crucial safeguard, ensuring that businesses can continue to operate and meet customer demands even when faced with unexpected challenges. It provides a buffer against the inherent uncertainties of the supply chain, allowing businesses to maintain continuity of operations and avoid costly disruptions.

Understanding Internal and External Demand: The Dual Nature of JIT

To appreciate the importance of safety stock in JIT systems, it's crucial to understand the distinction between internal and external demand.

- **External demand** refers to the demand for finished goods from customers. This demand is typically driven by market forces, consumer preferences, seasonality, and other external factors. It's the demand that ultimately drives revenue and profitability for the business.

- **Internal demand** refers to the demand for components, raw materials, or subassemblies within the production process. This demand is driven by the production schedule and the need to ensure that each stage of the production process has the necessary inputs to continue operating smoothly. It's the demand that keeps the wheels of production turning and ensures that finished goods are available to meet external demand.

In a JIT system, both internal and external demand must be carefully balanced. While the goal is to minimize inventory levels, it's equally important to ensure that each stage of the production process has enough inventory to avoid disruptions. This is where safety stock plays a crucial role, acting as a bridge between internal and external demand and ensuring that the production process can continue uninterrupted even in the face of unexpected fluctuations or delays.

The Kanban System: A Visual Representation of JIT and Safety Stock

The Kanban system, a core component of many JIT implementations, provides a visual and tangible representation of how safety stock functions within a lean manufacturing environment. In a Kanban system, work-in-process inventory is held in designated containers or bins, each with a Kanban card that signals when it's time to replenish the inventory.

When a downstream process consumes inventory from a bin, the empty bin and its Kanban card are sent back to the upstream process as a signal to produce or replenish the inventory. This creates a pull system, where production is driven by actual demand rather than forecasts, minimizing the risk of overproduction and excess inventory.

Safety stock is built into the Kanban system by maintaining a minimum number of Kanban cards for each item. This ensures that there's always a buffer stock available to meet unexpected demand or to cover for any delays in replenishment. The Kanban system provides a visual and intuitive way to manage inventory levels, making it easier to identify potential shortages and take corrective action before they impact production.

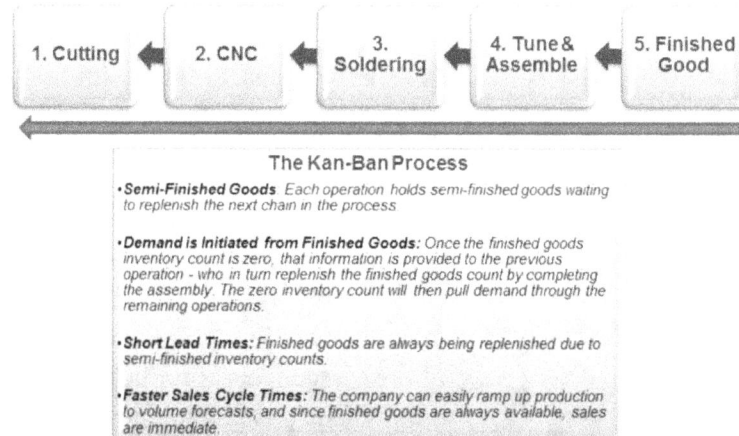

The Kan-Ban Process

- **Semi-Finished Goods** *Each operation holds semi-finished goods waiting to replenish the next chain in the process*

- **Demand is Initiated from Finished Goods:** *Once the finished goods inventory count is zero, that information is provided to the previous operation - who in turn replenish the finished goods count by completing the assembly. The zero inventory count will then pull demand through the remaining operations.*

- **Short Lead Times:** *Finished goods are always being replenished due to semi-finished inventory counts.*

- **Faster Sales Cycle Times:** *The company can easily ramp up production to volume forecasts, and since finished goods are always available, sales are immediate.*

The Costs of Low Inventory vs. the Costs of Holding Inventory: Striking the Right Balance

While the goal of JIT is to minimize inventory levels, it's important to recognize that there are costs associated with both having too much inventory and not having enough.

- **Costs of Holding Inventory:** These include a range of expenses, both tangible and intangible.

  - **Storage Costs** encompass warehouse rent, utilities, maintenance, security, and the labor costs of warehouse staff. These costs can escalate quickly, especially for businesses with large inventory volumes or those storing goods in prime locations.

o **Capital Costs** represent the opportunity cost of investing capital in inventory instead of other ventures that could potentially yield higher returns. This cost can be significant, especially for businesses with high-value inventory or limited access to capital.

o **Other Costs** include insurance premiums to protect against loss or damage, taxes on inventory held in stock, and the risk of obsolescence as products become outdated or unsellable due to technological advancements, changes in fashion, or other factors. Additionally, there's the potential for losses due to damage, theft, or spoilage of inventory.

- **Costs of Low Inventory:** The consequences of not having enough inventory can be far-reaching and impact various aspects of the business.

o **Lost Sales:** The most immediate and obvious cost is lost sales. When a customer is ready to buy but the product is out of stock, the sale is lost, along with the potential profit. This can significantly impact a company's revenue and profitability.

o **Expedited Freight Charges:** To fulfill urgent customer orders or replenish depleted inventory quickly, businesses often resort to expedited shipping, which can be significantly more expensive than standard shipping rates.

o   **Production Delays:** In manufacturing environments, stockouts of raw materials or components can lead to production delays, resulting in missed deadlines, lost productivity, and potential penalties from customers or partners.

o   **Loss of Customer Loyalty and Market Share:** Repeated stockouts can erode customer trust and loyalty, leading them to switch to competitors. This can result in a loss of market share and long-term revenue decline.

o   **Damage to Brand Reputation:** Stockouts can create a negative perception of your brand, as customers might view it as unreliable or unable to meet their needs. This can have long-lasting consequences for your company's image and future growth prospects.

The key to effective inventory management lies in finding the optimal balance between these two types of costs. This is where safety stock comes in. By maintaining a buffer inventory, businesses can mitigate the risks and costs associated with low inventory levels while still adhering to the principles of lean manufacturing.

Calculating Safety Stock: A Balancing Act

Determining the appropriate level of safety stock requires careful consideration of several factors, including:

- **Demand Variability:** The more volatile the demand for a product, the higher the safety stock needed to buffer against unexpected spikes. Analyzing historical sales data and understanding market trends can help you estimate demand variability and set appropriate safety stock levels.

- **Lead Time Uncertainty:** The longer and more unpredictable the lead time for replenishment, the higher the safety stock required to ensure product availability during potential delays. Factors such as supplier reliability, transportation disruptions, and customs clearance can impact lead times.

- **Service Level Targets:** The desired level of customer service also influences safety stock levels. Higher service levels, meaning a lower tolerance for stockouts, require more safety stock to ensure product availability.

Various statistical methods and formulas can be used to calculate safety stock, taking into account these factors and the company's risk tolerance. It's important to regularly review and adjust safety stock levels based on changing market conditions and demand patterns.

Technology's Role in Managing Safety Stock

Modern inventory management software and ERP systems can play a crucial role in managing safety stock effectively. These tools can help businesses:

- **Track Inventory Levels in Real-Time:** Monitor inventory levels across multiple locations and identify potential stockouts before they occur, enabling proactive replenishment.

- **Forecast Demand:** Utilize advanced forecasting techniques, such as machine learning algorithms or predictive analytics, to predict future demand more accurately and adjust safety stock levels accordingly.

- **Optimize Reorder Points:** Calculate optimal reorder points based on demand, lead times, and safety stock levels, ensuring timely replenishment without overstocking.

- **Automate Replenishment:** Generate automated purchase orders when inventory levels reach the reorder point, streamlining the procurement process and reducing administrative overhead.

- **Analyze Performance:** Track key performance indicators (KPIs) like inventory turnover, service levels, and carrying costs to identify areas for improvement and optimize inventory management strategies.

By leveraging technology, businesses can streamline their inventory management processes, improve accuracy, and make data-driven decisions that optimize safety stock levels and minimize costs.

Technology can also provide valuable insights into demand patterns, supplier performance, and other factors that can influence safety stock requirements.

Addressing Common Misconceptions About Safety Stock

Despite its importance, safety stock is often misunderstood and even viewed negatively by some proponents of lean manufacturing. Let's address some common misconceptions:

- **Safety Stock is Waste:** While excess inventory is indeed considered waste in JIT systems, safety stock serves a crucial purpose in mitigating the risks and costs associated with stockouts and production disruptions. It's not about holding unnecessary inventory but rather about maintaining a strategic buffer to ensure business continuity and customer satisfaction.

- **Safety Stock is a Sign of Inefficiency:** Some view safety stock as an indication of poor planning or forecasting. However, it's important to recognize that even the most sophisticated forecasting models can't predict every eventuality. Safety stock is a proactive measure to address the inherent uncertainties of the supply chain, not a reflection of inefficiency.

- **Safety Stock is Expensive:** While safety stock does incur carrying costs, these costs are often far outweighed by the potential costs of stockouts, such as lost sales, expedited freight charges, production delays, and damaged customer relationships. Safety stock is an investment in resilience and customer satisfaction, not an unnecessary expense.

Conclusion: Embracing Safety Stock as a Strategic Asset

In the pursuit of lean operations, it's easy to fall into the trap of viewing safety stock as a necessary evil or even a form of waste. However, the reality is that safety stock is a strategic asset that can protect businesses from the costly consequences of stockouts, production delays, and lost customer loyalty.

By understanding the role of safety stock in JIT systems, accurately calculating safety stock levels, and leveraging technology to manage inventory effectively, businesses can achieve the delicate balance between efficiency and responsiveness. This allows them to meet customer demands, minimize costs, and thrive in today's dynamic and unpredictable marketplace.

Remember, safety stock is not a sign of inefficiency; it's a testament to a company's preparedness and resilience. By embracing safety stock as a strategic asset, businesses can navigate the complexities of the supply chain with confidence, ensuring that they're always ready to meet the challenges and opportunities that lie ahead.

In the words of renowned management consultant Peter Drucker, "Efficiency is doing things right; effectiveness is doing the right things." By incorporating safety stock into your JIT system, you're not just doing things right—you're doing the right things to ensure the long-term success and sustainability of your business.

Chapter 12: Should You Negotiate Restocking Fees With B2B Customers? Accounting for Carrying Costs on Product Returns

Introduction: The B2B Returns Dilemma - A Costly Balancing Act

Picture this: a manufacturer of precision machine parts receives a large order from a key client. The order is customized to the client's exact specifications, requiring weeks of meticulous engineering and production. However, just as the shipment is ready to leave the warehouse, the client calls with a change of plans. The project has been delayed, and they no longer need the parts. Now, the manufacturer is left with a dilemma: accept the return and incur significant carrying costs, or refuse the return and risk damaging a valuable customer relationship.

This scenario highlights the complexities of product returns in the business-to-business (B2B) marketplace. Unlike the consumer world, where "no-hassle, money-back guarantees" are the norm, B2B transactions often involve customized products, longer sales cycles, and higher stakes. Accepting returns without any financial repercussions can be a costly proposition for businesses, tying up valuable resources and impacting profitability.

According to a study by the Reverse Logistics Association, the average cost of processing a return in the B2B sector is 15-20% of the product's value. This includes expenses related to transportation, inspection, repackaging, restocking, and potential loss of value due to obsolescence or damage. For businesses operating on thin margins, these costs can significantly erode profitability.

The Unique Challenges of B2B Returns

Several factors contribute to the complexities of product returns in the B2B realm, making them distinct from their B2C counterparts:

- **Customization:** B2B products are often customized or tailored to specific customer requirements, making them difficult to resell or repurpose if returned. This can lead to significant losses for the vendor, as they might have to scrap the returned items or incur additional costs to modify them for resale.

- **Longer Sales Cycles:** B2B sales cycles tend to be longer than B2C transactions, meaning returned products may have been in inventory for a considerable time, increasing the risk of obsolescence. Technological advancements or changes in market trends can render returned products outdated or less valuable, further impacting the vendor's profitability.

- **Higher Value:** B2B products are often more expensive than consumer goods, making the financial impact of returns more significant. A single returned item can represent a substantial loss for the vendor, especially if it's a high-value piece of equipment or machinery.

- **Complex Logistics:** Handling returns of large or specialized equipment can be logistically challenging and costly. This might involve arranging for specialized transportation, coordinating with third-party logistics providers, and ensuring proper handling and storage of the returned items.

These factors underscore the importance of carefully managing product returns in the B2B marketplace. While a lenient return policy might seem customer-friendly, it can have detrimental effects on a company's bottom line if not managed strategically.

Why Charge Restocking Fees?

Restocking fees serve as a deterrent to frivolous returns and help offset the costs associated with processing and restocking returned items. In the B2B context, these costs can be substantial.

- **Inspection and Testing:** Returned products often need to be inspected and tested to ensure they're in good working condition and meet quality standards before they can be restocked or resold. This process can involve labor costs, equipment usage, and potential disposal fees for damaged or non-conforming items.

- **Repackaging and Relabeling:** Returned items may need to be repackaged or relabeled before they can be put back into inventory or sold to another customer. This incurs additional labor and material costs.

- **Storage and Handling:** Returned products occupy valuable warehouse space and require handling, adding to storage and labor costs. This can be particularly challenging for businesses with limited warehouse capacity or those dealing with bulky or specialized items.

- **Obsolescence Risk:** The longer a returned product sits in inventory, the higher the risk of it becoming obsolete or losing value due to technological advancements or market changes. This can lead to significant losses for the vendor, especially for products with short lifecycles or rapidly evolving technologies.

- **Opportunity Cost of Capital:** The capital tied up in returned inventory represents a lost opportunity to invest in other areas of the business. This cost, while often intangible, can be significant, especially for businesses with limited financial resources.

By charging restocking fees, businesses can recoup some of these costs and discourage customers from making unnecessary returns. It also sends a message that the company values its products and services and expects customers to make informed purchasing decisions.

Calculating Restocking Fees: A Fair and Transparent Approach

Determining the appropriate restocking fee requires a careful analysis of the costs associated with processing and restocking the returned item. A simple three-step approach can help businesses calculate a fair and reasonable restocking fee:

1. **Calculate Initial Carrying Costs:** This includes the costs incurred to store and maintain the product from the time it was purchased to the time it was returned. These costs can include storage fees, insurance, and the opportunity cost of capital tied up in the inventory.

2. **Estimate New Carrying Costs:** This involves projecting the costs of storing and maintaining the returned product until it's resold. Factors to consider include the expected time to resell, potential price reductions due to depreciation or the need to offer discounts, and any additional handling or repackaging costs.

3. **Factor in Other Costs:** Include any original shipping costs to the customer, if applicable, as well as a percentage to cover overhead costs associated with processing the return, such as customer service, accounting, and logistics. These overhead costs are often overlooked but can add up

significantly, especially for businesses with high return volumes.

By adding these three components, you can arrive at a restocking fee that reflects the true cost of accepting the return. It's important to be transparent with customers about how the fee is calculated and the specific costs it covers. This transparency can help foster trust and understanding, reducing the likelihood of disputes or negative customer experiences.

When to Negotiate Restocking Fees: Flexibility and Customer Relationships

While restocking fees are a valuable tool for managing returns and protecting profitability, there are situations where negotiation might be appropriate. Flexibility in applying restocking fees can be a strategic move to maintain positive customer relationships and foster loyalty.

Consider being flexible on restocking fees if:

- **The product has a high inventory turnover rate:** If the returned product is in high demand and likely to be resold quickly, you might consider reducing or waiving the restocking fee to maintain a positive customer relationship. This demonstrates goodwill and shows the customer that you value their business.

- **The return is due to a product defect or error on your part:** If the return is a result of a product defect or an error in fulfilling the order, it's generally good practice to waive the restocking fee and take responsibility for the issue. This helps maintain customer satisfaction and reinforces your commitment to quality and service.

- **The customer is a key account or has a long-standing relationship with your company:** In some cases, it might be strategically beneficial to waive or reduce the restocking fee for valuable customers to maintain their loyalty and encourage future business. This can be seen as an investment in the relationship, fostering goodwill and demonstrating your commitment to their success.

When negotiating restocking fees, it's important to be transparent about your cost structure and the reasons behind the fee. Explain to the customer how the fee helps offset the costs associated with processing the return and ensure that your business remains profitable. By fostering open communication and demonstrating a willingness to work with the customer, you can reach a mutually agreeable solution that protects both parties' interests.

Beyond Restocking Fees: Alternative Solutions

While restocking fees are a common practice in B2B transactions, they're not the only solution for managing product returns. Consider exploring alternative approaches that might be more suitable for certain situations or customer relationships:

- **Store Credit:** Offer store credit instead of a refund, encouraging the customer to make future purchases from your company. This can help retain revenue and foster customer loyalty.

- **Exchanges:** Allow customers to exchange the returned product for a different item, potentially avoiding the need for a restocking fee. This can be a good option if the customer simply wants a different product or if the returned item is in good condition and can be easily resold.

- **Repair Services:** If the returned product is defective, offer repair services instead of a refund or exchange. This can help salvage the sale, maintain customer satisfaction, and potentially generate additional revenue from repair fees.

- **Consignment Inventory:** For certain products or industries, consider implementing a consignment inventory model, where the vendor retains ownership of the inventory until it's sold by the customer. This can reduce the risk of returns and associated costs for both parties.

The choice of which approach to adopt will depend on various factors, including the nature of the product, the reason for the return, and the value of the customer relationship. It's essential to have a clear return policy in place and to communicate it effectively to customers to avoid misunderstandings and disputes.

Technology and Automation: Streamlining the Returns Process

Technology can play a crucial role in streamlining the returns process and automating restocking fee calculations. Inventory management software and ERP systems can track returned items, calculate restocking fees based on predefined rules, and generate invoices or credit memos automatically. This not only saves time and reduces administrative overhead but also ensures consistency and accuracy in applying restocking fees.

Furthermore, technology can help identify patterns in returns, such as frequent returns from specific customers or product categories. This information can be used to proactively address underlying issues, such as product quality problems or inadequate customer training, and reduce the overall volume of returns.

Customer Communication: Setting Clear Expectations

Clear and transparent communication with customers is essential for managing product returns effectively. This involves clearly outlining your return and restocking fee policies on your website, invoices, and other relevant documents. Ensure that customers understand the terms and conditions of returns before they make a purchase. This includes specifying the timeframe for returns, any restrictions on eligible products, and the restocking fee percentage or calculation method.

When a customer requests a return, communicate the restocking fee clearly and explain the reasons behind it. This can help avoid misunderstandings and disputes later on. Be empathetic and understanding of the customer's situation, but also firm and consistent in enforcing your return policy.

Additionally, consider providing proactive communication to customers about your products and services to minimize the likelihood of returns. This could involve offering detailed product descriptions, specifications, and images, as well as providing training or support to ensure customers understand how to use your products correctly.

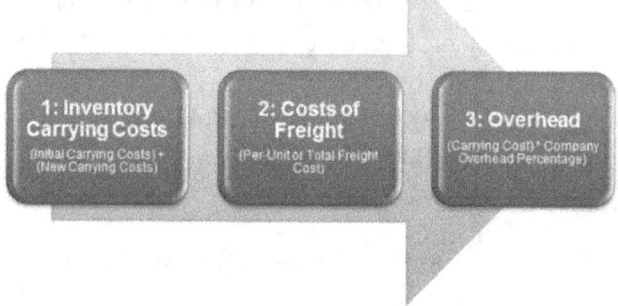

The Customer Perspective: Addressing Concerns and Objections

While restocking fees can be a valuable tool for businesses, it's important to acknowledge the customer's perspective. Some customers might view restocking fees as unfair or punitive, especially if they're accustomed to the lenient return policies prevalent in the B2C market.

To address these concerns, it's crucial to:

- **Emphasize the Value:** Clearly communicate the value your company provides and the costs associated with processing returns. Explain how restocking fees help cover these costs and ensure that your business remains profitable, allowing you to continue providing high-quality products and services.

- **Offer Alternatives:** In some cases, it might be beneficial to offer alternative solutions to restocking fees, such as store credit or exchanges. This can help maintain customer satisfaction and encourage future purchases.

- **Be Flexible:** Consider negotiating restocking fees for valuable customers or in situations where the return is due to a product defect or error on your part. This demonstrates goodwill and fosters a positive customer relationship.

- **Educate Customers:** Proactively educate customers about your return and restocking fee policies. This can help set clear expectations and reduce the likelihood of disputes or negative experiences.

By addressing customer concerns and demonstrating a willingness to work with them, you can maintain positive relationships while still protecting your company's profitability.

Conclusion: A Balanced Approach to Returns Management

Managing product returns in the B2B marketplace is a complex and multifaceted challenge. While it's important to be accommodating to customers, it's equally crucial to protect your company's profitability. Restocking fees can be a valuable tool for achieving this balance, but they should be implemented strategically and with clear communication.

By understanding the unique challenges of B2B returns, accurately calculating restocking fees, and being willing to negotiate when appropriate, businesses can manage returns effectively while maintaining positive customer relationships. Remember, the goal is not to penalize customers but to ensure that the costs associated with returns are fairly shared and that your business remains profitable.

In conclusion, adopting a balanced approach to returns management involves:

- **Clear Policies:** Establish clear and transparent return and restocking fee policies that are communicated effectively to customers.

- **Accurate Costing:** Calculate restocking fees based on the actual costs associated with processing and restocking returned items.

- **Flexibility and Negotiation:** Be willing to negotiate restocking fees in certain situations to maintain customer relationships and foster loyalty.

- **Technology and Automation:** Leverage technology to streamline the returns process and automate restocking fee calculations.

- **Customer Communication:** Prioritize clear and proactive communication with customers regarding your return and restocking fee policies.

By implementing these strategies, businesses can navigate the complexities of B2B returns, protect their profitability, and build stronger, more sustainable customer relationships. Remember, effective returns management is not just about minimizing costs; it's also about maximizing customer satisfaction and fostering long-term loyalty.

Chapter 13: Inventory Stock Outs: The Hidden Costs of Transportation-Out Freight and COGS

Introduction: The Silent Erosion of Profit Margins

In the intricate world of inventory management, there exists a prevailing belief that lower inventory levels always translate to lower costs. This mindset, often driven by the pursuit of lean operations and efficiency, can lead businesses down a treacherous path. While reducing excess inventory can undoubtedly free up capital and minimize storage costs, it's crucial to recognize the potential pitfalls of being *too* lean. When inventory levels dip below the optimal point, a cascade of hidden costs can emerge, silently eroding profit margins and jeopardizing customer satisfaction.

The Domino Effect of Stockouts: A Cautionary Tale

Imagine a bustling e-commerce warehouse during the peak holiday season. Orders are pouring in, but the shelves are alarmingly bare. The website flashes "out of stock" messages, frustrating customers and driving them to competitors. Meanwhile, on a factory floor, production lines grind to a halt as a critical component runs out of stock. The silence is deafening, as workers stand idle, deadlines loom, and the company faces the prospect of missed deliveries and financial losses.

These scenarios, while hypothetical, paint a vivid picture of the tangible and often painful consequences of low inventory levels. The impact isn't limited to the immediate loss of sales; it sets off a chain reaction that can reverberate throughout the entire organization. Customer relationships are strained, brand reputation suffers, and operational efficiency plummets.

The financial repercussions of stockouts are equally alarming. According to a study by IHL Group, stockouts cost retailers a staggering $634.1 billion annually in lost sales worldwide. This figure underscores the immense financial impact of inventory shortages. But the costs of low inventory extend far beyond missed sales opportunities. They can ripple through the entire organization, affecting customer relationships, operational efficiency, and overall profitability.

In this chapter, we'll embark on a journey to uncover the often-overlooked costs associated with low inventory levels, particularly the hidden expenses of transportation-out freight and their impact on the cost of goods sold (COGS). We'll challenge conventional accounting practices, explore the nuances of cost allocation in stockout scenarios, and offer insights into how businesses can gain a more accurate picture of their true profitability.

Transportation-In Versus Transportation-Out: A Conventional Divide

Traditional accounting practices draw a clear distinction between transportation-in and transportation-out costs. Transportation-in costs, which include the expenses incurred to bring goods into the company's warehouse or facility, are typically included in the cost of goods sold (COGS). This makes intuitive sense, as these costs are directly associated with acquiring the inventory that will eventually be sold to customers.

On the other hand, transportation-out costs, which encompass the expenses of delivering goods to customers, are generally treated as a separate expense, often categorized as a selling expense or a cost of sales. This approach is logical when delivery is considered a service provided by the company, such as in the case of e-commerce retailers or businesses offering free shipping.

However, the traditional distinction between transportation-in and transportation-out costs becomes blurred when a company incurs outbound freight expenses due to an inventory stockout. In such scenarios, the company is not providing a standard delivery service but rather taking extraordinary measures to fulfill an order that should have been readily available.

Challenging the Status Quo: Accounting for Stockout-Related Freight Costs

Let's consider a scenario where a manufacturer receives an urgent order from a key client. Unfortunately, the required product is out of stock due to a recent surge in demand or unforeseen supply chain disruptions. To avoid losing the sale and jeopardizing the customer relationship, the manufacturer expedites a shipment from their supplier and then incurs additional freight costs to deliver the product to the customer on time.

In this case, the transportation-in costs associated with the expedited shipment from the supplier would likely be included in the COGS. However, the transportation-out costs incurred to deliver the product to the customer might be treated as a separate expense, not directly reflected in the COGS. This can create a distorted picture of the true cost of the sale, as it fails to account for the additional expenses incurred due to the stockout.

While adhering to established accounting principles is important, it's equally crucial to recognize the potential blind spots in traditional cost allocation methods. In the context of inventory stockouts, treating outbound freight costs as a separate expense can mask the true financial impact of inventory shortages. It reinforces the misconception that inventory only costs money when you have it, while ignoring the often-significant costs associated with not having enough inventory to meet demand.

To gain a more accurate understanding of the true cost of goods sold, it's worth considering incorporating transportation-out freight costs incurred due to stockouts into the COGS calculation. This approach acknowledges that these costs are directly related to the sale of the product and should be factored into its overall cost.

The Two Categories of Inventory Costs: A Balancing Act

To gain a more comprehensive understanding of inventory costs, it's helpful to categorize them into two main groups:

1. **Carrying Costs:** These are the costs associated with holding inventory. They include a range of expenses, both tangible and intangible.

    o **Storage Costs** encompass warehouse rent, utilities, maintenance, security, and the labor costs of warehouse staff. These costs can escalate quickly, especially for businesses with large inventory volumes or those storing goods in prime locations. Efficient warehouse management practices, such as optimizing space utilization and implementing automation technologies, can help minimize these costs.

- o **Capital Costs** represent the opportunity cost of investing capital in inventory instead of other ventures that could potentially yield higher returns. This cost can be significant, especially for businesses with high-value inventory or limited access to capital. It's essential to consider the potential return on investment for alternative uses of capital when evaluating inventory carrying costs.

- o **Other Costs:** Holding costs also include insurance premiums to protect against loss or damage, taxes on inventory held in stock, and the risk of obsolescence as products become outdated or unsellable due to technological advancements, changes in fashion, or other factors. Additionally, there's the potential for losses due to damage, theft, or spoilage of inventory. Proper handling procedures, security measures, and regular inventory audits can help mitigate these risks.

2. **Stockout Costs:** These are the costs incurred when a company runs out of stock. They can be both direct and indirect, impacting various aspects of the business.

o   **Lost Sales:** The most immediate and obvious cost is lost sales. When a customer is ready to buy but the product is out of stock, the sale is lost, along with the potential profit. This can significantly impact a company's revenue and profitability. To quantify the impact of lost sales, businesses can calculate the potential revenue lost based on historical sales data and estimated demand.

o   **Expedited Freight Charges:** To fulfill urgent customer orders or replenish depleted inventory quickly, businesses often resort to expedited shipping, which can be significantly more expensive than standard shipping rates. These additional freight costs can eat into profit margins and negatively impact the bottom line.

o   **Production Delays:** In manufacturing environments, stockouts of raw materials or components can lead to production delays, resulting in missed deadlines, lost productivity, and potential penalties from customers or partners. These delays can disrupt the entire supply chain and have a cascading effect on downstream operations.

o   **Loss of Customer Loyalty and Market Share:** Repeated

stockouts can erode customer trust and loyalty, leading them to switch to competitors. In today's hyper-competitive marketplace, where customers have countless options, a single negative experience can trigger a permanent loss of business. This can result in a loss of market share and a decline in long-term revenue.

- o **Damage to Brand Reputation:** Stockouts can create a negative perception of your brand, as customers might view it as unreliable or unable to meet their needs. This can have long-lasting consequences for your company's image and future growth prospects, as negative word-of-mouth and online reviews can spread quickly and damage your brand's credibility.

Effective inventory management involves striking a delicate balance between these two types of costs. Carrying too much inventory leads to high carrying costs, while carrying too little inventory can result in costly stockouts. The goal is to find the optimal inventory level that minimizes the total cost of both carrying and stockout costs.

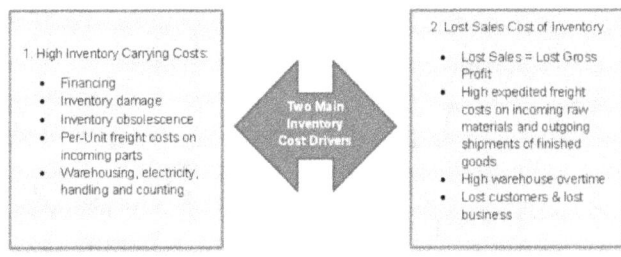

1. High Inventory Carrying Costs:

- Financing
- Inventory damage
- Inventory obsolescence
- Per-Unit freight costs on incoming parts
- Warehousing, electricity, handling and counting

Two Main Inventory Cost Drivers

2. Lost Sales Cost of Inventory

- Lost Sales = Lost Gross Profit
- High expedited freight costs on incoming raw materials and outgoing shipments of finished goods
- High warehouse overtime
- Lost customers & lost business

The Role of Safety Stock: A Buffer Against Uncertainty

One effective strategy for mitigating the risk of stockouts and their associated costs is to maintain safety stock. Safety stock is an additional quantity of inventory held in reserve to protect against unexpected fluctuations in demand or supplier lead times.

By having safety stock on hand, businesses can ensure that they have enough inventory to meet customer demands even if there are unforeseen delays or spikes in orders. This can help prevent lost sales, reduce the need for expedited shipments, and maintain customer satisfaction. It acts as a buffer, providing a cushion against the inherent uncertainties of the supply chain and ensuring that businesses can continue to operate smoothly even when faced with unexpected challenges.

Calculating the appropriate level of safety stock requires careful consideration of several factors:

- **Demand Variability:** The more volatile the demand for a product, the higher the safety stock needed to buffer against unexpected spikes. Analyzing historical sales data, understanding market trends, and considering seasonality factors can help you estimate demand variability and set appropriate safety stock levels.

- **Lead Time Uncertainty:** The longer and more unpredictable the lead time for replenishment, the higher the safety stock required to ensure product availability during potential delays. Factors such as supplier reliability, transportation disruptions, and customs clearance can impact lead times. It's essential to factor in these uncertainties when determining safety stock levels.

- **Service Level Targets:** The desired level of customer service also influences safety stock levels.

Higher service levels, meaning a lower tolerance for stockouts, require more safety stock to ensure product availability. Businesses need to balance the cost of carrying safety stock with the potential costs of stockouts and the desired level of customer service.

Various statistical methods and formulas can be used to calculate safety stock, taking into account these factors and the company's risk tolerance. Some common methods include:

- **Standard Deviation Method:** This method uses the standard deviation of demand during the lead time to calculate safety stock. It assumes that demand follows a normal distribution and provides a certain level of confidence that stockouts will not occur.

- **Service Level Method:** This method calculates safety stock based on the desired service level, which represents the probability of not experiencing a stockout during the lead time. Higher service levels require more safety stock.

- **Simulation:** This method uses computer simulations to model various demand and lead time scenarios to determine the optimal safety stock level that minimizes the total cost of inventory management.

It's important to regularly review and adjust safety stock levels based on changing market conditions and demand patterns. This ensures that your safety stock remains adequate to protect against potential disruptions without incurring excessive carrying costs.

Integrating Transportation-Out Costs into COGS: A More Accurate Picture

To gain a more accurate picture of the true cost of goods sold, it's worth considering incorporating transportation-out freight costs incurred due to stockouts into the COGS calculation. This approach acknowledges that these costs are directly related to the sale of the product and should be factored into its overall cost.

While this might deviate from traditional accounting practices, it provides a more realistic representation of the financial impact of inventory shortages. By including stockout-related freight costs in the COGS, businesses can make more informed decisions about inventory levels, pricing strategies, and customer service levels. It also highlights the true cost of stockouts and encourages businesses to take proactive measures to prevent them.

Technology's Role in Inventory Optimization

Modern inventory management software and ERP systems can play a crucial role in optimizing inventory levels, tracking costs, and mitigating the risks of stockouts. These tools can help businesses:

- **Track Inventory Levels in Real-Time:** Monitor inventory levels across multiple locations and identify potential stockouts before they occur, enabling proactive replenishment. This real-time visibility allows businesses to respond quickly to changes in demand and avoid costly disruptions.

- **Forecast Demand:** Utilize advanced forecasting techniques, such as machine learning algorithms or predictive analytics, to predict future demand more accurately and adjust inventory levels accordingly. By leveraging historical sales data, market trends, and other relevant factors, businesses can improve their forecasting accuracy and reduce the risk of both stockouts and overstocks.

- **Optimize Reorder Points:** Calculate optimal reorder points based on demand, lead times, and safety stock levels, ensuring timely replenishment without overstocking. This helps maintain optimal inventory levels and minimize carrying costs.

- **Automate Replenishment:** Generate automated purchase orders when inventory levels reach the reorder point, streamlining the procurement process and reducing administrative overhead. Automation can also help reduce the risk of human error and ensure timely replenishment.

- **Analyze Performance:** Track key performance indicators (KPIs) like inventory turnover, service levels, and carrying costs to identify areas for improvement and optimize inventory management strategies. By analyzing these metrics, businesses can gain insights into their inventory performance and make data-driven decisions to improve efficiency and profitability.

By leveraging technology, businesses can gain greater visibility into their supply chain, make data-driven decisions, and proactively manage inventory levels to minimize the risk of stockouts and their associated costs. Technology can also enable better collaboration with suppliers, improve demand forecasting accuracy, and streamline the entire inventory management process.

Conclusion: A Holistic Approach to Inventory Management

Effective inventory management is not just about minimizing carrying costs or avoiding stockouts; it's about finding the optimal balance between these two competing forces. By understanding the true costs of low inventory, including the often-hidden expenses of transportation-out freight, businesses can make more informed decisions about their inventory strategies.

The EOQ model provides a valuable framework for calculating the ideal order quantity, but it's essential to adapt it to your specific business context and consider real-world complexities like demand variability and lead time uncertainty. By incorporating safety stock, leveraging technology, and fostering collaboration across departments, businesses can achieve inventory equilibrium, minimize costs, and enhance customer satisfaction.

Remember, inventory management is an ongoing process that requires constant vigilance and adaptation. By staying attuned to market trends, customer demands, and supply chain dynamics, you can ensure that your inventory strategy remains effective and supports your business's long-term success.

In conclusion, the costs of low inventory can be significant and far-reaching. From lost sales and high freight costs to decreased profit margins, damaged customer relationships, and lost market share, the consequences of being too lean can ripple through the entire organization. By understanding these costs and implementing proactive inventory management strategies, businesses can avoid these pitfalls and achieve a sustainable balance between efficiency and customer satisfaction.

The EOQ model, while not a perfect solution, provides a valuable framework for optimizing inventory levels and minimizing costs. By adapting the model to your specific business context, leveraging technology, and fostering collaboration across departments, you can achieve inventory equilibrium and position your business for long-term success.

Remember that inventory management is not just about numbers and formulas; it's about understanding your business, your customers, and your supply chain dynamics. It's about striking the perfect balance between efficiency and responsiveness, ensuring that you have the right products, in the right quantities, at the right time, to meet the ever-changing demands of the market and delight your customers.

Chapter 14: Warehouse Carrying Costs Per Square Foot: Three Simple Steps to Unveiling Hidden Costs

Introduction: The Silent Drain on Warehouse Profitability

Imagine a sprawling warehouse, meticulously organized with rows upon rows of shelves stacked high with inventory. It's a picture of efficiency and productivity, but beneath the surface lies a hidden cost that can silently erode a company's profitability: warehouse carrying costs.

These costs, often overlooked or underestimated, encompass a wide range of expenses associated with storing and maintaining inventory. From warehouse rent and utilities to insurance premiums and the risk of obsolescence, these costs can quickly add up, impacting a company's bottom line.

Understanding and managing warehouse carrying costs is crucial for any business that relies on physical inventory. It's not just about knowing the total cost of storing goods; it's about understanding the cost per square foot of warehouse space occupied by inventory. This metric provides valuable insights into the true cost of holding inventory and can guide businesses in making informed decisions about inventory levels, warehouse space utilization, and pricing strategies.

In this chapter, we'll explore a simple yet effective three-step process for calculating warehouse carrying costs per square foot. We'll go beyond the traditional approach of simply dividing warehouse expenses by square footage, delving into the specific costs associated with holding inventory for extended periods. By understanding these costs and their impact on your business, you can take proactive steps to optimize your inventory management practices and boost your bottom line.

Beyond Simple Storage Costs: Understanding the True Cost of Carrying Inventory

Most approaches to calculating warehouse costs involve taking your yearly warehouse expenses and dividing them by the total square footage. For instance, if your company spent $900,000 on warehousing (including rent, utilities, employee salaries, equipment, insurance, etc.) and had a 100,000-square-foot warehouse, your cost per square foot would be $9.

While this provides a basic understanding of storage costs, it doesn't capture the full picture of inventory carrying costs. Carrying costs encompass a broader range of expenses that go beyond just the physical storage of goods. They include:

- **Capital Costs:** The opportunity cost of capital tied up in inventory, representing the potential return on investment if that capital were used elsewhere in the business.

- **Storage Costs:** Warehouse rent, utilities, maintenance, security, and labor costs associated with storing inventory.

- **Obsolescence Costs:** The cost of inventory becoming outdated or unsellable due to technological advancements, changes in fashion, or other factors.

- **Damage and Shrinkage Costs:** Losses due to damage, theft, or spoilage of inventory.

- **Insurance Costs:** Premiums paid to insure inventory against loss or damage.

- **Handling Costs:** Expenses related to moving, picking, and packing inventory.

- **Taxes:** Any applicable taxes on inventory held in stock.

These costs can vary significantly depending on the industry, product type, market conditions, and a company's specific inventory management practices. Therefore, it's crucial to go beyond simple storage costs and calculate your company's specific carrying costs to gain a more accurate picture of the true cost of holding inventory.

Three Simple Steps to Calculate Warehouse Carrying Costs Per Square Foot

To determine your warehouse carrying costs per square foot, follow these three simple steps:

Step 1: Determine Your Specific Inventory Costs

Many companies apply a standard 3% monthly inventory carrying cost to the inventory value on hand. For example, if your average monthly inventory value is $1 million, your monthly carrying costs would be $30,000, translating to $360,000 annually.

However, your company's carrying costs could be higher or lower than this industry average. Factors such as the nature of your products, your storage practices, and your risk management strategies can all influence your carrying costs.

To get a more accurate picture, it's essential to break down your carrying costs into their individual components. This includes analyzing expenses related to financing, storage, obsolescence, damage, theft, insurance, handling, and taxes. By identifying the specific cost drivers within your business, you can gain a deeper understanding of where your money is going and identify opportunities for cost reduction.

Utilize tools like Excel spreadsheets or inventory management software to track and calculate your carrying costs. This will allow you to define your company's specific costs of holding products on your shelves and gain valuable insights into your inventory management practices.

Step 2: Yearly Carrying Costs Divided by Square Footage

Once you've determined your yearly carrying costs, divide this amount by the total square footage of your warehouse. For example, if your yearly carrying costs are $350,000 and your warehouse is 100,000 square feet, your carrying cost per square foot would be $3.50.

This metric provides a clear picture of how much it costs your company to hold inventory per square foot of warehouse space. It can be used to evaluate the efficiency of your warehouse layout, identify areas for improvement, and make informed decisions about inventory levels and storage strategies.

Step 3: Focus on Reducing Costs

The final step is to leverage the insights gained from your carrying cost analysis to identify and implement strategies for cost reduction. By understanding your specific cost drivers, you can target areas where you can make the most significant impact on your bottom line.

Some effective strategies for reducing carrying costs per square foot include:

- **Improving Inventory Turnover:** The faster you sell your inventory, the less time it spends in your warehouse, reducing carrying costs. Focus on improving demand forecasting, optimizing pricing strategies, and streamlining your sales and marketing efforts to increase sales velocity.

- **Minimizing Damage, Obsolescence, and Theft:** Implement proper handling procedures, invest in security measures, and adopt inventory management practices that minimize the risk of damage, obsolescence, and theft. This can include regular inventory audits, cycle counting, and proper storage and rotation of goods.

- **Liquidating Slow-Moving Inventory:** Identify slow-moving or obsolete items and take proactive steps to liquidate them through discounts, promotions, or other sales channels. This frees up valuable warehouse space and reduces carrying costs associated with holding onto stagnant inventory.

- **Optimizing Warehouse Space Utilization:** Evaluate your warehouse layout and storage practices to ensure efficient use of space. Consider implementing vertical storage solutions, optimizing picking and packing processes, and utilizing technology like warehouse management systems to improve space utilization and reduce handling costs.

- **Negotiating with Suppliers:** Work with your suppliers to negotiate better payment terms, consignment inventory arrangements, or other strategies that can help reduce your carrying costs.

- **Outsourcing:** Consider outsourcing warehousing or logistics functions to third-party providers who can leverage economies of scale and expertise to offer more cost-effective solutions.

By implementing these and other cost-reduction strategies, you can significantly lower your carrying costs per square foot and improve your overall profitability.

Real-World Success: A Case Study

Let's look at a real-world example of how a company successfully reduced its warehouse carrying costs per square foot. A mid-sized electronics distributor was struggling with high inventory levels and escalating carrying costs. They decided to conduct a thorough analysis of their inventory and warehouse operations, using the three-step process outlined in this chapter.

Through this analysis, they discovered that a significant portion of their carrying costs was due to slow-moving and obsolete inventory. They also identified inefficiencies in their warehouse layout and storage practices.

Armed with these insights, the company implemented a series of changes. They introduced a more rigorous demand forecasting process, implemented a just-in-time inventory system for their fast-moving items, and liquidated their slow-moving and obsolete inventory through targeted promotions. They also reorganized their warehouse layout and invested in new storage solutions to optimize space utilization.

As a result of these efforts, the company was able to reduce its carrying costs per square foot by 25%, freeing up valuable capital and improving its overall profitability. They also saw improvements in customer satisfaction due to reduced stockouts and faster order fulfillment.

This was this individual's graph that came from performing the second step of this three step process.

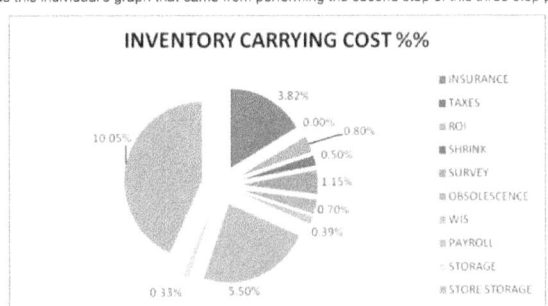

Conclusion: Turning Warehouse Costs into a Competitive Advantage

Understanding and managing warehouse carrying costs per square foot is essential for any business that relies on physical inventory. By going beyond simple storage costs and analyzing the true cost of holding inventory, businesses can identify areas for improvement and implement strategies to reduce expenses and boost profitability.

The three-step process outlined in this chapter provides a practical framework for calculating and optimizing warehouse carrying costs. By diligently tracking your inventory costs, identifying cost drivers, and implementing targeted cost-reduction strategies, you can transform your warehouse from a cost center into a source of competitive advantage.

Remember, effective inventory management is an ongoing process. Continuously monitor your inventory levels, track your costs, and adapt your strategies as needed to stay ahead of the curve and ensure your business thrives in today's dynamic marketplace. By mastering the art and science of inventory optimization, you can unlock hidden profits, improve operational efficiency, and position your business for long-term success.

Chapter 15: Operating with Razor-Thin Profit Margins? Reduce Financing Costs and Boost Profits

Introduction: The High-Stakes Game of Thin Margins

In the fiercely competitive business landscape, operating with razor-thin profit margins is akin to navigating a treacherous financial tightrope. Every fluctuation in costs, every delay in payment, every unforeseen expense can tip the scales and send a company tumbling into the red. For businesses in this precarious position, managing finances isn't merely a matter of bookkeeping—it's a matter of survival. The slightest misstep can have far-reaching consequences, impacting everything from growth potential to employee morale.

The impact of thin profit margins is particularly pronounced when it comes to financing costs. Even minor changes in interest rates can have a cascading effect on a company's ability to generate profit.

Moreover, long receivables collection times, where customers delay payments, can further exacerbate the financial strain, creating a cash flow crunch that can stifle growth and innovation.

However, for companies grappling with the challenges of large receivables and payables, there's a silver lining. By strategically leveraging these financial instruments and adopting a proactive approach to financial management, businesses can unlock hidden opportunities to reduce financing costs, improve cash flow, and ultimately bolster their bottom line. In this chapter, we'll delve into the intricacies of managing finances in a thin-margin environment, exploring various strategies and tactics that companies can employ to navigate the financial tightrope and achieve sustainable profitability.

The Value of the $1.00 Profit Rule: A Simple Yet Powerful Concept

To truly appreciate the impact of financing costs on profitability, let's consider the "$1.00 profit rule." This simple yet powerful concept highlights the leverage that reducing financing costs can have on a company's bottom line, especially for those operating with thin margins.

The $1.00 profit rule states that for every dollar saved in financing costs, it's equivalent to generating a certain amount of sales revenue needed to achieve the same profit. The exact amount varies depending on the company's profit margin. For instance, if a company's profit margin is 10%, saving $1 in financing costs is equivalent to generating $10 in sales revenue. This illustrates the disproportionate impact that even small reductions in financing costs can have on profitability.

Reducing Financing Costs: A Multifaceted Approach

Reducing financing costs is not a one-time event but an ongoing process that requires a multifaceted approach. It's not just about securing lower interest rates; it's about optimizing various aspects of your operations that influence your financial health. Let's explore some key strategies that businesses can employ to achieve this:

1. Inventory Financing: Turning Inventory into a Cash Flow Asset

Inventory often represents a significant portion of a company's assets, tying up valuable capital that could be used for other purposes. By optimizing inventory levels and implementing effective financing strategies, businesses can reduce the financial burden of carrying inventory and improve their cash flow.

- **Just-in-Time (JIT) Inventory:** JIT is a widely adopted inventory management strategy that aims to minimize inventory levels by receiving goods only as they are needed for production or sale. This can significantly reduce carrying costs, such as storage expenses, insurance premiums, and the risk of obsolescence. However, JIT requires precise demand forecasting, reliable supplier relationships, and robust supply chain management capabilities.

- **Consignment Inventory:** In this arrangement, the supplier retains ownership of the inventory until it's sold by the buyer. This allows the buyer to defer payment until the goods are sold, improving cash flow and reducing carrying costs. Consignment inventory can be a valuable tool for businesses with limited working capital or those operating in industries with long sales cycles.

- **Vendor-Managed Inventory (VMI):** In a VMI model, the vendor assumes responsibility for managing inventory levels at the customer's location. This can lead to improved inventory control, reduced stockouts, and optimized replenishment, benefiting both the vendor and the customer. VMI requires a high level of trust and collaboration between the two parties, but it can lead to significant cost savings and improved efficiency.

- **Inventory Financing:** For businesses that require additional working capital to finance inventory purchases, inventory financing can be a viable option. This involves securing a loan or line of credit specifically for inventory purchases, allowing businesses to maintain adequate stock levels without straining their cash flow. However, it's essential to carefully evaluate the terms and interest rates associated with inventory financing to ensure it's a cost-effective solution.

- **Evaluating Inventory Turnover:** Inventory turnover is a key metric that measures how efficiently a company manages its inventory. A high inventory turnover ratio indicates that a company is selling its inventory quickly, which can help reduce carrying costs and improve cash flow. Businesses can calculate their inventory turnover ratio by dividing the cost of goods sold by the average inventory value.

Month	Price	QTY	Your Costs	Gross Profit/Sale	Gross Profit % (Before Rebate)	Customer's Rebate/Unit	Customer's Bank Total / Transaction	Gross Profit % (After Rebate)
Jan	$12.10	10	$7.00	$5.10	42%	$0.25	$2.50	40%
Feb	$12.10	10	$7.00	$5.10	42%	$0.25	$2.50	40%
Mar	$12.10	10	$7.00	$5.10	42%	$0.25	$2.50	40%
Apr	$11.75	10	$7.00	$4.75	40%	$0.25	$2.50	38%
May	$11.75	10	$7.00	$4.75	40%	$0.25	$2.50	38%
June	$11.60	10	$7.00	$4.60	40%	$0.25	$2.50	38%
July	$11.60	10	$7.00	$4.60	40%	$0.25	$2.50	38%
Aug	$11.60	10	$7.00	$4.60	40%	$0.25	$2.50	38%
Sept	$11.50	10	$7.00	$4.50	39%	$0.25	$2.50	37%
Oct	$11.50	10	$7.00	$4.50	39%	$0.25	$2.50	37%
Nov	$11.50	10	$7.00	$4.50	39%	$0.25	$2.50	37%
Dec	$11.50	10	$7.00	$4.50	39%	$0.25	$2.50	37%
						Customer's Bank	$30.00	

2. Receivables Management: Accelerating Cash Inflows

Efficient receivables management is crucial for maintaining healthy cash flow and reducing financing costs. By accelerating the collection of outstanding invoices, businesses can reduce their reliance on external financing and improve their financial flexibility.

- **Invoicing and Payment Terms:** Clearly define your invoicing and payment terms, and communicate them effectively to customers. Consider offering early payment discounts to incentivize prompt payment.

This can help accelerate cash inflows and reduce the need for external financing.

- **Credit Policies:** Establish clear credit policies and procedures to assess customer creditworthiness and minimize the risk of bad debts. Regularly review and update your credit policies to reflect changing market conditions and customer behavior. Consider using credit scoring models or other tools to assess credit risk and make informed decisions about extending credit to customers.

- **Collections Process:** Implement a proactive and efficient collections process to follow up on overdue invoices and resolve payment issues promptly. This might involve sending reminder emails, making phone calls, or even engaging a collections agency in extreme cases. A well-defined collections process can help reduce the average collection period and improve cash flow.

- **Alternative Financing:** If your business faces cash flow challenges due to long receivables collection times, consider alternative financing options like invoice factoring or discounting. These solutions allow you to access cash quickly by selling your outstanding invoices to a third-party financing company. While these options come with fees, they can be a valuable tool for bridging cash flow gaps and avoiding the need for more expensive forms of financing.

- **Analyzing Days Sales Outstanding (DSO):** DSO is a key metric that measures the average number of days it takes a company to collect payment after a sale. A high DSO indicates that a company is taking longer to collect its receivables, which can negatively impact cash flow. By tracking and analyzing DSO, businesses can identify areas for improvement in their collections process and take steps to accelerate cash inflows.

Existing Financing on COGS: Cost of Goods Sold	
Yearly Interest Rate	6.00%
Daily Interest Rate	0.0164%
Product's COGS	$ 10,000.00
Daily Cost to Finance COGS	$ 1.64
Days to Collect on Invoice	45
Total Cost of Financing	$ 73.97

Receivable Factoring based on Invoice/Receivable Value	
Receivable's Total Value	$ 15,000.00
Factoring Advance	80%
Total Advance	$ 12,000.00
Administration Fee	1.00%
Total Cost of Administration Fee (fee * receivable)	$ 150.00
Prime Rate	3.00%
Flat or tiered fee	3.00%
Total Rate (Prime + Flat)	6.00%
Effective Daily Rate	0.0164%
Daily Cost of Factoring (effective daily rate * advance)	$ 1.97260
Days to Collect on Invoice	45
Days to Finance factoring	$ 88.77
Total Costs of Factorin: Financing + Administration Fee	$ 238.77

3. Leasing Large Capital Expenditures: Preserving Cash and Flexibility

For businesses operating with thin profit margins, investing in large capital expenditures can be a significant financial burden. Leasing equipment or machinery instead of purchasing them outright can be a smart strategy to preserve cash and maintain financial flexibility.

Leasing offers several advantages:

- **Lower Upfront Costs:** Leasing typically requires lower upfront payments compared to purchasing, freeing up capital for other investments or operational expenses. This can be particularly beneficial for businesses with limited cash reserves or those looking to avoid taking on additional debt.

- **Predictable Payments:** Lease payments are usually fixed, making it easier to budget and manage cash flow. This predictability can help businesses avoid unexpected expenses and maintain financial stability.

- **Tax Benefits:** In many cases, lease payments may be tax-deductible as operating expenses, reducing your overall tax burden. Consult with a tax advisor to understand the specific tax implications of leasing in your jurisdiction.

- **Flexibility:** Leasing allows you to upgrade or replace equipment more easily as technology evolves or your business needs change. This can be particularly valuable in industries where technology is rapidly advancing or where equipment obsolescence is a concern.

However, it's essential to carefully evaluate the terms of any lease agreement and compare it to the cost of ownership before making a decision. Consider factors such as the lease duration, interest rates, any potential penalties or fees for early termination or excessive wear and tear, and the option to purchase the equipment at the end of the lease term.

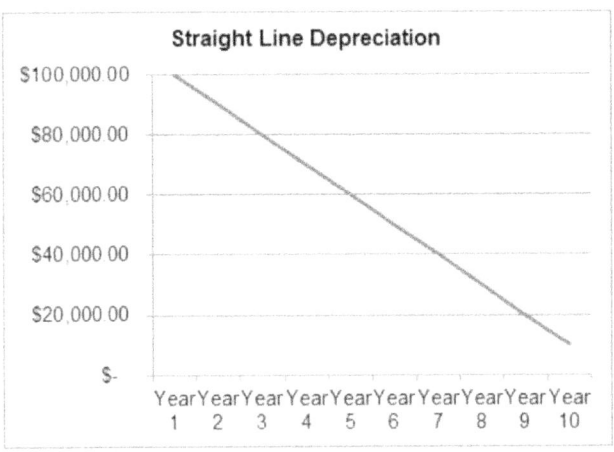

Straight Line Depreciation

4. Negotiating with Lenders and Suppliers: Leveraging Your Buying Power

Don't be afraid to negotiate with your lenders and suppliers to secure more favorable terms and pricing. If you have a good credit history and a strong track record of timely payments, you may be able to negotiate lower interest rates on loans or lines of credit.

Similarly, if you're a significant buyer or have the potential for repeat business, leverage that buying power to negotiate better pricing and payment terms with your suppliers. This could involve asking for volume discounts, extended payment terms, or other concessions that can help reduce your financing costs and improve your cash flow.

Remember, negotiation is a two-way street. Be prepared to offer something in return for the concessions you're seeking. This could involve committing to a larger order volume, providing testimonials or referrals, or offering to pay invoices early in exchange for a discount.

5. Streamlining Operations and Reducing Waste: Efficiency is Key

Efficiency is paramount for businesses operating with thin profit margins. By streamlining your operations and eliminating waste, you can reduce costs, improve productivity, and enhance your bottom line.

This might involve:

- **Lean Manufacturing:** Implementing lean manufacturing principles to identify and eliminate waste in your production processes. This could involve reducing inventory levels, optimizing workflows, and improving quality control.

- **Process Improvement:** Continuously evaluating and improving your workflows to identify bottlenecks and inefficiencies. This could involve automating tasks, eliminating unnecessary steps, and empowering employees to suggest improvements.

- **Technology Adoption:** Leveraging technology to automate tasks, improve communication, and streamline operations. This could involve implementing inventory management software, utilizing data analytics to gain insights into your operations, and adopting cloud-based solutions to improve collaboration and accessibility.

- **Employee Training and Development:** Investing in your employees' skills and knowledge to enhance their productivity and efficiency. This could involve providing training on new technologies, processes, or best practices, as well as offering opportunities for professional development and growth.

By creating a culture of continuous improvement and focusing on eliminating waste, businesses can achieve significant cost savings and improve their overall financial health. This not only helps them navigate the challenges of thin profit margins but also positions them for long-term success and growth.

Conclusion: Navigating the Path to Profitability

Operating with razor-thin profit margins is undoubtedly challenging, but it's not insurmountable. By adopting a proactive and strategic approach to financial management, businesses can navigate this high-stakes game and achieve sustainable profitability.

Reducing financing costs is a crucial piece of the puzzle. By optimizing inventory levels, accelerating cash inflows, leveraging leasing options, negotiating favorable terms, and streamlining operations, businesses can free up valuable capital, improve cash flow, and boost their bottom line.

Remember, every dollar saved in financing costs translates to increased profit margins. By focusing on these key areas and continuously seeking opportunities for improvement, you can navigate the financial tightrope with confidence and achieve long-term success.

In the end, it's not just about surviving with thin profit margins; it's about thriving and building a resilient business that can weather any economic storm. By implementing these strategies and fostering a culture of financial discipline and innovation, you can position your company for continued growth and prosperity.

The path to profitability might be narrow, but with careful planning, strategic execution, and a relentless focus on efficiency, businesses can overcome the challenges of thin margins and achieve sustainable success. Remember, it's not just about cutting costs; it's about creating value, building strong relationships, and making smart financial decisions that empower your business to reach its full potential.

Chapter 16: Five B2B Strategies That Balance Inventory Carrying Costs and Low Inventory Counts

Introduction: The Delicate Dance of Inventory Management

In the intricate world of business, the pursuit of profit often involves walking a tightrope between conflicting objectives. One such tightrope is the delicate balance between minimizing inventory carrying costs and ensuring adequate stock levels to meet customer demand and avoid lost sales. The former calls for a lean approach, minimizing inventory to free up capital and reduce storage expenses. The latter necessitates a buffer stock to ensure product availability and avoid stockouts, which can lead to missed sales opportunities and dissatisfied customers.

Finding this equilibrium is a challenge for businesses of all sizes, but it's particularly crucial for those operating with razor-thin profit margins. In such scenarios, even minor fluctuations in inventory costs or sales can have a significant impact on the bottom line. The stakes are high, but the rewards of effective inventory management are equally substantial. By striking the right balance, businesses can optimize their inventory levels, reduce costs, improve customer satisfaction, and enhance their overall profitability.

The tension between procurement and sales departments often exacerbates this challenge. Procurement aims to minimize inventory costs, while sales seeks to ensure product availability to meet customer demand. This conflict can lead to suboptimal inventory levels and missed opportunities.

In this chapter, we will explore five key strategies that can help businesses navigate this delicate dance and achieve a harmonious balance between inventory carrying costs and low inventory counts. We will delve into the nuances of each strategy, providing real-world examples, actionable tips, and insights to empower businesses to make informed decisions and optimize their inventory management practices.

1. Long-Term Contractual Agreements: Securing Predictability and Shared Responsibility

Long-term contractual agreements with customers can be a powerful tool for balancing inventory carrying costs and ensuring product availability. These agreements provide a sense of predictability, allowing businesses to forecast demand more accurately and align their inventory levels accordingly.

- **Types of Agreements and Their Benefits:**

Several types of long-term contracts can be utilized, each offering unique advantages:

- **Blanket Orders:** These agreements outline a commitment from the customer to purchase a certain quantity of goods over a specified period, typically at a discounted price. This allows the supplier to plan their production and inventory levels more effectively, reducing the risk of overstocks or stockouts. It also provides the customer with price stability and ensures product availability.

- **Master Service Agreements (MSAs):** MSAs establish the general terms and conditions governing future transactions between a buyer and a seller. They streamline the procurement process by eliminating the need to negotiate individual contracts for each purchase. This can save time and resources for both parties while ensuring consistency and predictability in their business dealings.

- **Framework Agreements:** These agreements establish a framework for future contracts between a buyer and multiple suppliers. They typically outline the terms and conditions for a specific category of goods or services, such as IT equipment or consulting services. Framework agreements can simplify procurement processes, promote competition among suppliers, and ensure compliance with standardized terms.

- **Negotiating Carrying Costs:** When entering into long-term contracts, it's crucial to address the issue of inventory carrying costs. This involves negotiating provisions that outline how these costs will be shared or allocated between the buyer and the supplier. Factors to consider during negotiations include:

  - **Inventory Age:** The longer the inventory remains unsold, the higher the carrying costs. Consider including provisions that incentivize the customer to take ownership of the inventory sooner or share the carrying costs after a certain period.

  - **Storage Requirements:** If the products require specialized storage conditions, such as refrigeration or climate control, these costs should be factored into the agreement.

  - **Market Conditions:** The volatility of the market and the potential for price fluctuations should be considered when negotiating carrying cost provisions.

- **Case Study: A Win-Win Partnership**

A leading electronics manufacturer entered into a long-term contractual agreement with a major retailer. The agreement included a provision for shared carrying costs, where the retailer would contribute a percentage of the holding costs for inventory that remained unsold after a certain period. This arrangement incentivized the retailer to promote the manufacturer's products aggressively and ensure timely sales, while the manufacturer benefited from reduced carrying costs and increased sales volume.

2. Stronger Vendor Agreements: Forging Strategic Alliances

Just as long-term agreements with customers can help balance inventory costs, so too can stronger vendor agreements. By collaborating closely with suppliers and establishing clear expectations, businesses can optimize their inventory levels, reduce carrying costs, and enhance supply chain efficiency.

- **Supplier Evaluation and Selection:** The foundation of strong vendor agreements lies in careful supplier evaluation and selection. Choose suppliers based not only on price but also on their reliability, quality, financial stability, and ability to support your inventory management goals. Consider factors like lead times, on-time delivery rates, quality control processes, and their willingness to collaborate on inventory management initiatives.

- **Collaborative Planning, Forecasting, and Replenishment (CPFR):** CPFR is a collaborative process where buyers and suppliers work together to align their demand forecasts and inventory plans. This involves sharing information on sales data, promotions, and other factors that can influence demand. By working together, both parties can achieve greater visibility into the supply chain, improve forecasting accuracy, and optimize inventory levels.

• **Vendor Performance Metrics and Incentives:** Establish clear performance metrics and incentives for suppliers, rewarding those who consistently deliver on time, meet quality standards, and actively participate in inventory management initiatives. This can help foster a culture of accountability and continuous improvement within your supplier network.

• **Technology-Enabled Collaboration:** Leverage technology solutions like supplier portals and electronic data interchange (EDI) to facilitate seamless communication and data sharing with your suppliers. This can improve visibility, streamline processes, and enable real-time collaboration on inventory management.

Inventory Costs Without Agreements

Quarterly Inventory	Inventory Retained	Per-Unit Cost	Finished Goods	Monthly Carryin costs	Total Cost of Ownership
Month 1	12000	$ 5.00	$ 60,000.00	3%	$ 1,800.00
Month 2	10000	$ 5.00	$ 50,000.00	3%	$ 1,500.00
Month 3	15000	$ 5.00	$ 75,000.00	3%	$ 2,250.00
					$ 5,550.00

Inventory Costs With Shared Burden

Quarterly Inventory	Inventory Retained	Per-Unit Cost	Finished Goods	Monthly Carryin costs	Total Cost of Ownership
Month 1	12000	$ 5.00	$ 60,000.00	1.50%	$ 900.00
Month 2	10000	$ 5.00	$ 50,000.00	1.50%	$ 750.00
Month 3	15000	$ 5.00	$ 75,000.00	1.50%	$ 1,125.00
					$ 2,775.00

3. Inventory Liquidations: Turning Stale Stock into Cash

One of the biggest contributors to high carrying costs is slow-moving or obsolete inventory. Holding onto these items in the hopes of eventually selling them at full price is a recipe for financial loss. The longer these items sit on your shelves, the more they depreciate in value, incur storage costs, and tie up valuable capital that could be invested elsewhere.

To mitigate this risk, businesses need to adopt a proactive approach to inventory liquidation. This involves identifying slow-moving or obsolete items and taking decisive action to sell them, even if it means offering discounts or accepting a lower profit margin. The goal is to recoup some of the invested capital and free up valuable warehouse space.

Some effective strategies for liquidating outdated inventory include:

- **Discount Sales and Promotions:** Offer discounts or bundle deals to incentivize customers to purchase slow-moving items. This can help generate cash flow and clear out excess inventory.

- **Clearance Sales:** Hold periodic clearance sales to attract bargain hunters and quickly move outdated or excess inventory.

- **Donation or Recycling:** If the items are no longer sellable, consider donating them to charity or recycling them responsibly. This can generate goodwill and potentially offer tax benefits.

- **Online Marketplaces:** Utilize online marketplaces or liquidation platforms to reach a wider audience and sell excess inventory quickly.

- **Technology-Enabled Liquidation:** Leverage inventory management software and analytics tools to identify slow-moving items and automate liquidation processes, such as setting dynamic pricing or triggering alerts for clearance sales.

By proactively managing slow-moving and outdated inventory, businesses can free up valuable warehouse space, improve cash flow, and reduce carrying costs. It's essential to have a clear liquidation strategy in place and to act decisively when inventory starts to stagnate.

4. Asset Management Strategy (Inventory Analyst Position): Treating Inventory as a Valuable Asset

Adopting an asset management mindset towards inventory can be a game-changer for businesses seeking to balance carrying costs and low inventory counts. This approach involves treating inventory as a valuable asset that needs to be managed strategically to maximize its value and minimize its costs.

One effective way to implement an asset management strategy is to create an inventory analyst position within your organization. This individual would be responsible for:

- **Tracking Inventory Performance:** Analyzing inventory turnover rates, identifying slow-moving items, and monitoring carrying costs. This involves regularly reviewing inventory data, identifying trends, and generating reports to inform decision-making.

- **Forecasting Demand:** Utilizing historical sales data, market trends, and other relevant information to predict future demand and optimize inventory levels. This requires a combination of statistical analysis, market research, and collaboration with sales and marketing teams.

- **Collaborating with Sales and Procurement:** Working closely with the sales and procurement teams to align inventory levels with sales forecasts and procurement plans. This ensures that the right products are available at the right time to meet customer demand without incurring excessive carrying costs.

- **Implementing Cost-Reduction Strategies:** Identifying and implementing strategies to reduce carrying costs, such as optimizing warehouse space utilization, improving inventory turnover, and minimizing damage and obsolescence. This involves a continuous evaluation of inventory management practices and a willingness to embrace new technologies and approaches.

By having a dedicated inventory analyst, businesses can gain a deeper understanding of their inventory performance, identify areas for improvement, and make data-driven decisions to optimize their inventory management practices. This can lead to significant cost savings, improved efficiency, and enhanced customer satisfaction.

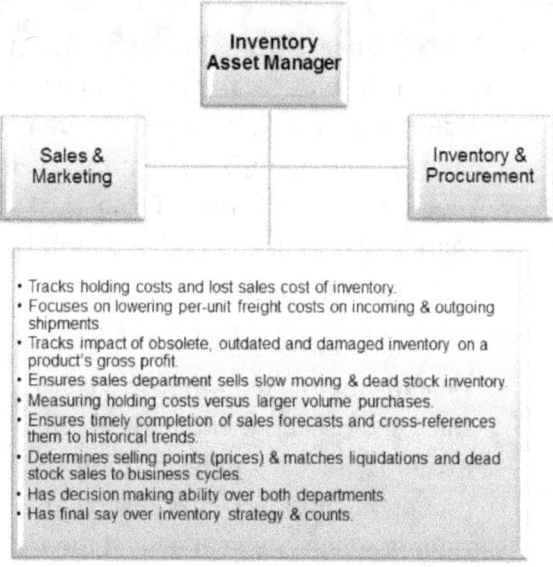

Inventory Asset Manager

Sales & Marketing

Inventory & Procurement

- Tracks holding costs and lost sales cost of inventory.
- Focuses on lowering per-unit freight costs on incoming & outgoing shipments.
- Tracks impact of obsolete, outdated and damaged inventory on a product's gross profit.
- Ensures sales department sells slow moving & dead stock inventory.
- Measuring holding costs versus larger volume purchases.
- Ensures timely completion of sales forecasts and cross-references them to historical trends.
- Determines selling points (prices) & matches liquidations and dead stock sales to business cycles.
- Has decision making ability over both departments.
- Has final say over inventory strategy & counts.

5. Measure Procurement's Performance on Gross Profit: Aligning Incentives

Traditionally, procurement teams have been evaluated based on their ability to reduce purchase prices. However, this narrow focus can lead to unintended consequences, such as sacrificing quality for lower prices or neglecting other important factors that contribute to overall profitability.

To ensure that procurement decisions align with the company's broader financial goals, it's essential to measure their performance based on gross profit objectives. This involves considering not just the purchase price but also other factors that impact profitability, such as:

- **Inventory Carrying Costs:** The costs associated with holding inventory, as discussed earlier in this chapter. These costs include storage, capital, insurance, obsolescence, damage, and theft. By factoring in carrying costs, procurement teams are encouraged to make purchasing decisions that not only minimize the upfront cost but also consider the long-term financial implications of holding inventory.

- **Supplier Performance:** The reliability and responsiveness of suppliers, including their ability to meet delivery deadlines and quality standards, can significantly impact a company's profitability. Late deliveries or defective products can lead to production delays, stockouts, and customer dissatisfaction, all of which can erode profit margins. By evaluating suppliers based on their performance, procurement teams can ensure a reliable and efficient supply chain that supports the company's financial goals.

- **Total Cost of Ownership (TCO):** The TCO encompasses the overall cost of acquiring, using, and disposing of a product or service, including not just the purchase price but also factors like maintenance, repair, and disposal costs. By considering the TCO, procurement teams can make more informed decisions about which suppliers and products offer the best long-term value, even if their upfront costs might be slightly higher.

By aligning procurement's performance metrics with gross profit objectives, businesses can encourage them to make decisions that not only reduce costs but also contribute to overall profitability. This might involve negotiating favorable payment terms with suppliers, implementing vendor-managed inventory programs, or focusing on sourcing high-quality materials that minimize the risk of defects and returns. It also fosters a collaborative environment where procurement works in tandem with other departments, such as sales and marketing, to achieve shared goals and maximize the company's financial performance.

Conclusion: Achieving Inventory Equilibrium

Finding the balance between high inventory carrying costs and low inventory counts is a complex challenge, but it's essential for businesses seeking to optimize their operations and maximize profitability. The strategies outlined in this chapter, from long-term contractual agreements and stronger vendor partnerships to inventory liquidation and asset management, can help businesses navigate this delicate dance and achieve inventory equilibrium.

Remember, effective inventory management is not just about minimizing costs; it's also about maximizing customer satisfaction and ensuring that your business has the right products, in the right quantities, at the right time. By adopting a holistic approach to inventory management and leveraging the power of collaboration, technology, and data-driven decision-making, you can transform your supply chain into a source of competitive advantage and achieve sustainable growth in today's dynamic marketplace.

In conclusion, striking the perfect balance between inventory carrying costs and low inventory counts requires a multifaceted approach that considers various factors, including demand forecasting, supplier relationships, cost analysis, and technology utilization. By implementing the strategies discussed in this chapter and continuously evaluating and refining your inventory management practices, you can optimize your inventory levels, reduce costs, improve customer satisfaction, and ultimately drive greater profitability and success for your business.

Chapter 17: Sales Strategies Versus Purchasing Strategies: Your Sales & Procurement Team Can Help Each Other in Negotiation

Introduction: Bridging the Gap for Greater Profitability

In the intricate dance of business operations, sales and procurement teams often find themselves on seemingly opposite sides of the stage. Sales, the revenue generators, are driven by the pursuit of maximizing profits through successful deals and expanding market share. Procurement, the cost custodians, are tasked with minimizing expenses and securing the best possible deals from suppliers. This inherent conflict can sometimes lead to a disconnect between the two functions, resulting in missed opportunities and suboptimal outcomes for the company as a whole.

However, what if we reimagine this dynamic not as a clash but as a potential synergy? What if sales and procurement, instead of operating in silos, could leverage each other's expertise and insights to enhance negotiation skills and ultimately boost the company's bottom line?

The reality is that sales and procurement share a common goal: to contribute to the company's profitability. While their approaches might differ, their ultimate objective is the same. By fostering collaboration and knowledge-sharing between these two functions, businesses can unlock a wealth of untapped potential and achieve greater success in negotiations.

The Interplay of Sales and Procurement: A Symbiotic Relationship

To understand the potential synergy between sales and procurement, let's examine how they approach price negotiations.

- **Sales Perspective:** The sales team focuses on protecting pricing by highlighting the product's features, benefits, and unique value proposition. They strive to differentiate their offering from competitors and convince customers that the price is justified based on the value they receive. They also need to be adept at handling customer objections and countering requests for discounts.

- **Procurement Perspective:** The procurement team, on the other hand, aims to reduce pricing by shifting the focus away from product features and benefits and towards competitive bidding and cost analysis. They leverage their knowledge of market prices, supplier capabilities, and alternative options to negotiate the best possible deal.

These contrasting perspectives offer a unique opportunity for mutual learning and growth. Sales teams can gain valuable insights into customer negotiation tactics, price sensitivity, and the factors that influence their purchasing decisions. Procurement teams can learn from sales' ability to articulate value propositions, handle objections, and build relationships with customers.

By bridging the gap between sales and procurement, businesses can create a more collaborative and effective negotiation environment. This can lead to improved outcomes for both functions, ultimately benefiting the company as a whole.

Reducing Training Costs and Enhancing Negotiation Skills: A Five-Step Process

Traditional sales and procurement training programs often focus on general negotiation strategies and tactics, lacking the specificity and context needed to address the unique challenges of each function. However, by fostering cross-functional training and knowledge sharing, businesses can create a more targeted and effective learning experience while also reducing training costs.

Here's a simple five-step process to enhance the negotiation skills of your sales and procurement teams:

1. **List of Sales Strategies:** Have your sales team compile a list of their most effective sales strategies, particularly those used to defend pricing against competitive offers. Encourage them to focus on highlighting the unique value proposition of your products or services and offering alternative solutions to price concessions. Additionally, have them list common customer concessions and how they typically handle them.

2. **List of Procurement Strategies:** Similarly, have your procurement team create a list of their negotiation strategies, particularly those aimed at shifting the focus away from product features and benefits and towards competitive pricing. Encourage them to share their tactics for analyzing market prices, leveraging supplier competition, and negotiating favorable terms. Also, have them list common vendor concessions and how they are addressed.

List of Sales Strategies
* Defend Price
* High Volume Orders
* Long-Term Contracts
* Cross-Selling
* Extended Lead Times

List of Procurement Strategies
* Reduce Prices
* Extended Terms
* Larger Credit
* Faster Delivery

3.   **Role-Play Negotiation:** Organize role-playing exercises where members of the sales and procurement teams take on the roles of buyers and sellers. Use scenarios that reflect real-world negotiations your company encounters. This allows both teams to practice their strategies, observe each other's tactics, and gain a deeper understanding of the negotiation process from different perspectives.

4.   **Debriefing:** After each role-play session, conduct a thorough debriefing. Discuss the strengths and weaknesses of each team's approach, analyze the negotiation dynamics, and identify areas for improvement. Encourage open communication and feedback, fostering a collaborative learning environment.

5.   **A New List of Concessions:** Based on the insights gained from the role-play and debriefing sessions, have both teams create a new list of concessions. The sales team's list should focus on concessions that reduce customer costs without lowering product prices, such as offering extended warranties, free training, or bundled services. The procurement team's list should focus on

concessions that can be used to reduce prices from vendors, such as volume discounts, extended payment terms, or improved delivery schedules.

Benefits of Cross-Functional Training

By implementing this cross-functional training approach, businesses can reap several benefits:

- **Reduced Training Costs:** Instead of relying solely on external trainers or consultants, businesses can leverage the expertise within their own organization, reducing training expenses.

- **Targeted and Relevant Learning:** The training is tailored to the specific needs and challenges faced by sales and procurement teams in your industry, making it more relevant and impactful.

- **Improved Negotiation Skills:** By learning from each other's perspectives and tactics, both teams can enhance their negotiation skills and achieve better outcomes in real-world scenarios.

- **Enhanced Collaboration:** Cross-functional training fosters a culture of collaboration and understanding between sales and procurement, leading to improved communication, aligned goals, and ultimately, increased profitability.

- **Increased Profitability:** By improving negotiation skills and aligning incentives, both sales and procurement teams can contribute to the company's bottom line.

Sales can protect profit margins by defending prices and offering value-added solutions, while procurement can reduce costs by securing better deals from suppliers.

Conclusion: Unlocking the Power of Collaboration

In the quest for profitability, businesses often overlook the potential synergies between their sales and procurement teams. By bridging the gap between these two functions and fostering a culture of collaboration and knowledge sharing, companies can unlock a wealth of untapped potential.

The five-step process outlined in this chapter provides a practical framework for implementing cross-functional training and enhancing negotiation skills. By encouraging sales and procurement teams to learn from each other, businesses can create a more cohesive and effective approach to negotiations, leading to improved outcomes, reduced costs, and increased profitability.

Remember, negotiation is not just about winning or losing; it's about finding solutions that work for everyone involved. By approaching negotiations with a collaborative mindset and a focus on creating value, both sales and procurement teams can contribute to the company's success and achieve their shared goal of maximizing profitability.

Chapter 18: When Should You Start a Strategic Business Unit (SBU)? Charting New Territories for Growth

Introduction: The SBU Conundrum - To Branch Out or Not?

In the ever-evolving landscape of business, the siren call of new markets beckons many companies. The allure of untapped opportunities, the prospect of reaching new customer segments, and the potential for exponential growth can be irresistible. Perhaps your company has identified a promising niche market, a disruptive technology, or a geographic region ripe for expansion. The vision of conquering new territories and reaping the rewards of increased revenue is enticing, but the path forward is not without its challenges.

Launching a new venture, especially one that diverges significantly from your core business, requires a substantial investment of time, resources, and personnel. It's a strategic decision that demands careful consideration and meticulous planning. How can you justify diverting resources from your existing operations to pursue an uncertain future? How can you ensure that this new venture aligns with your overall corporate strategy and contributes to your long-term vision?

For companies grappling with these questions, the concept of a Strategic Business Unit (SBU) offers a potential solution. An SBU is, in essence, a separate entity within the larger organization, possessing its own distinct cost structure, operations, marketing and sales functions, and strategic focus. It's designed to operate independently, catering to a specific market with unique customer segments, competitive landscape, and selling conditions.

The decision to establish an SBU is not to be taken lightly. It requires a thorough evaluation of the opportunity, a realistic assessment of the risks, and a well-defined strategy for execution. In this chapter, we'll explore the key considerations involved in deciding whether to launch an SBU, providing a roadmap for navigating the complexities of this strategic decision.

The Success of an SBU: Beyond the Size of the Parent Company

A common misconception is that strategic business units are the exclusive domain of large corporations with abundant resources and market clout. However, the reality is that any company, regardless of its size, can benefit from establishing an SBU if the opportunity aligns with its strategic goals and capabilities.

The success of an SBU hinges not on the size of the parent company but on the size and viability of the opportunity itself. It's about identifying a market with significant growth potential, where your product or service can address unmet needs or offer a unique value proposition. It's about assessing the competitive landscape and determining whether you have the resources and capabilities to compete effectively.

Moreover, it's crucial to consider whether success in this new market requires a dedicated and focused approach that might not be feasible within the existing organizational structure. If the answer to these questions is affirmative, then launching an SBU might be a strategic move worth considering.

Five Key Considerations for Launching an SBU

1. Define the Market's Size and Dynamics: Unveiling the Potential

Before venturing into a new market, it's imperative to conduct thorough market research to understand its size, growth potential, competitive landscape, and regulatory environment. This information will help you gauge the potential demand for your product or service and assess the feasibility of establishing an SBU.

- **Market Size and Growth:** Determine the current size of the target market and its projected growth rate. This information will help you estimate the potential revenue and market share your SBU could capture. Use a variety of sources, including industry reports, market research publications, government data, and online databases.

- **Customer Segmentation:** Identify the key customer segments within the market and their specific needs, preferences, and buying behavior. This will enable you to tailor your product or service offerings, marketing messages, and sales strategies to resonate with your target audience. Utilize tools like surveys, focus groups, and customer interviews to gain deeper insights into your potential customers.

- **Competitive Landscape:** Analyze the competitive landscape, identifying key players, their strengths and weaknesses, and their market share. This will help you understand the competitive dynamics and develop strategies to differentiate your SBU. Conduct a SWOT analysis (Strengths, Weaknesses, Opportunities, and Threats) to assess your SBU's position relative to competitors.

- **Regulatory Environment:** Research any relevant regulations, standards, or compliance requirements that might impact your operations in the new market. This includes import/export regulations, product safety standards, and any industry-specific regulations. Ensure that your SBU is prepared to meet all legal and regulatory requirements to avoid costly penalties or delays.

- **Market Trends:** Stay abreast of the latest trends and developments in the market, including technological advancements, shifting consumer preferences, and emerging competitors. This will help you anticipate changes and adapt your strategies accordingly. Subscribe to industry publications, attend conferences and trade shows, and monitor social media and online forums to stay informed about the latest developments.

Remember, market research is an ongoing process. As you gather more information and gain experience in the new market, you'll need to continuously refine your understanding and adapt your strategies accordingly.

Case Study: Nike's Expansion into the Skateboarding Market

In the early 2000s, Nike, a global leader in athletic footwear and apparel, recognized the growing popularity of skateboarding and the potential for expansion into this market. However, they also understood that the skateboarding culture was distinct from their traditional customer base, requiring a different approach to product design, marketing, and sales.

To address this challenge, Nike established a dedicated SBU, Nike SB, focused solely on the skateboarding market. They hired experienced skateboarders to design and develop products that resonated with the skateboarding community, and they partnered with influential skateboarders and skate shops to build brand awareness and credibility.

This strategic approach proved to be highly successful. Nike SB quickly gained traction in the skateboarding market, capturing a significant market share and contributing to Nike's overall growth. The SBU's success demonstrated the power of understanding a new market's unique dynamics and tailoring strategies accordingly.

2. Define the Opportunity: Clarity of Purpose

Once you have a solid understanding of the market, it's time to clearly define the opportunity your SBU will pursue. This involves answering key questions that will shape the SBU's strategy and direction:

- **What are you offering?** Are you introducing a new product to a new market, a new product to an existing market, or an existing product to a new market? Each scenario presents unique challenges and opportunities, requiring a tailored approach.

- **Who are your target customers?** Identify the specific customer segments within the market that you will focus on serving. What are their needs, pain points, and motivations? How does your product or service address these needs and provide value? Develop detailed customer personas to gain a deeper understanding of your target audience.

- **What is your competitive advantage?** What sets your product or service apart from existing offerings in the market? What unique value proposition can you offer to customers? Identify your key differentiators and leverage them to create a compelling brand positioning.

• **What is your pricing strategy?** How will you price your product or service? What factors will influence your pricing decisions, such as production costs, competitor pricing, and customer perceived value? Conduct a thorough pricing analysis to ensure your pricing is competitive and profitable.

• **What are your sales and marketing channels?** How will you reach your target audience and promote your product or service? What marketing and sales tactics will you employ to generate leads, convert prospects into customers, and build brand awareness? Develop a comprehensive marketing and sales plan that outlines your key channels, messaging, and tactics.

• **What are the potential barriers to entry?** What challenges might you face when entering the new market, such as regulatory hurdles, established competitors, or cultural differences? How will you overcome these barriers and establish a foothold in the market? Develop contingency plans and strategies to address potential challenges and mitigate risks.

By clearly defining the opportunity and answering these questions, you can create a focused and actionable business plan for your SBU. This plan will serve as a roadmap, guiding your decisions and actions as you navigate the complexities of entering a new market.

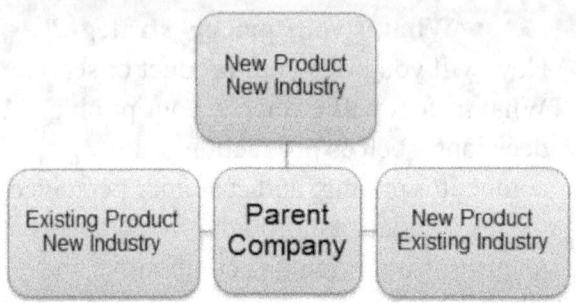

Example: Apple's Entry into the Smartphone Market

In 2007, Apple, then primarily known for its computers and music players, ventured into the burgeoning smartphone market with the launch of the iPhone. This marked a significant departure from their core business, requiring a dedicated SBU to focus on the unique challenges and opportunities of this new market.

Apple's SBU strategy involved:

- **Innovative Product:** The iPhone offered a revolutionary user experience with its touchscreen interface and intuitive operating system.

- **Targeted Marketing:** Apple's marketing campaigns focused on highlighting the iPhone's unique features and benefits, creating a sense of desire and aspiration among consumers.

- **Premium Pricing:** The iPhone was priced at a premium, reflecting its perceived value and exclusivity.

- **Selective Distribution:** Initially, Apple partnered with a single carrier, AT&T, to control distribution and maintain brand image.

This focused and strategic approach paid off handsomely. The iPhone quickly became a cultural phenomenon, disrupting the smartphone market and propelling Apple to new heights of success. The SBU's ability to identify a clear opportunity, develop a differentiated product, and execute a targeted marketing strategy played a pivotal role in its triumph.

3. Perform a Customer Needs Assessment: Understanding Your Target Audience

To succeed in a new market, it's not enough to simply have a great product or service; you need to have a deep understanding of your target customers' needs, preferences, and buying behavior. This requires conducting a customer needs assessment to gather insights into their pain points, challenges, and expectations.

- **Identify Key Decision-Makers:** In B2B markets, understanding the key decision -makers involved in the purchasing process is crucial. Who are the individuals or groups that influence or authorize the purchase of your product or service? What are their roles and responsibilities? What factors do they consider when making purchasing decisions? By understanding the key decision-makers, you can tailor your sales and marketing efforts to resonate with their needs and priorities.

- **Understand Pain Points and Challenges:** What are the key challenges or pain points that your target customers face? How does your product or service address these challenges and provide solutions? Conduct surveys, interviews, or focus groups to gather feedback from potential customers and gain insights into their unmet needs. Use this information to refine your product or service offerings and develop compelling marketing messages that highlight the value you provide.

- **Assess Preferences and Expectations:** What are your customers' preferences in terms of product features, pricing, delivery, and customer service? What level of service and support do they expect? Understanding these preferences allows you to tailor your offerings and create a customer experience that exceeds expectations.

- **Gauge Price Sensitivity:** How price-sensitive are your target customers? What is their budget for your product or service? How does your pricing compare to competitors? Conducting market research and analyzing competitor pricing can help you determine the optimal pricing strategy for your SBU.

By understanding your customers' needs and expectations, you can create a compelling value proposition that resonates with them. This involves tailoring your product or service offerings, marketing messages, and sales strategies to meet their specific requirements and address their pain points.

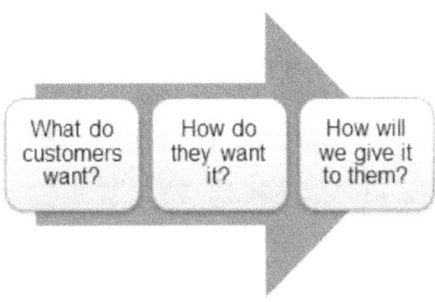

4. Determine Overhead and Cost Structure: Financial Viability

An SBU, while operating under the umbrella of the parent company, is essentially a separate entity with its own cost structure and overhead. It's crucial to carefully analyze and project the costs associated with establishing and running the SBU to ensure its financial viability.

This involves:

- **Personnel Costs:** Estimate the salaries, benefits, and other expenses associated with hiring the necessary staff for the SBU, including sales, marketing, operations, customer service, finance, and potentially, research and development. Consider the experience and expertise required for each role, as well as the prevailing salary levels in the target market. It's also important to factor in the costs of training and onboarding new employees.

- **Operational Costs:** Factor in the costs of office space, equipment, technology, utilities, and other operational expenses. These costs can vary significantly depending on the location, size, and scope of the SBU's operations. Conduct thorough research and obtain quotes from vendors to estimate these costs accurately. Consider leasing options for equipment or office space to reduce upfront capital expenditures.

- **Marketing and Sales Costs:** Allocate a budget for marketing and sales activities, such as advertising, promotions, trade shows, and sales commissions. The specific costs will depend on your target market, marketing channels, and sales strategies. Develop a detailed marketing and sales plan to estimate these costs and track your spending.

- **Overhead Costs:** Allocate a portion of the parent company's overhead costs to the SBU, such as rent, utilities, and administrative expenses. This ensures that the SBU bears its fair share of the company's overall operating costs. Use activity-based costing or other allocation methods to accurately assign overhead costs to the SBU.

By meticulously analyzing these costs, you can create a realistic budget for the SBU and assess its potential profitability. This will help you make informed decisions about resource allocation, pricing strategies, and the overall financial viability of the venture.

5. Define Gross Profit on Sales and Net Profit: The Bottom Line

Ultimately, the success of an SBU is measured by its ability to generate profit. It's essential to define your target gross profit on sales and net profit after expenses. This involves:

- **Pricing Strategy:** Determine your pricing strategy based on your cost structure, target market, and competitive landscape. Ensure that your prices are competitive while still allowing for a healthy profit margin. Consider factors such as customer price sensitivity, perceived value, and the potential for volume discounts. Conduct market research and competitor analysis to understand the prevailing pricing trends in the market.

- **Sales Forecast:** Develop a realistic sales forecast based on your market research and understanding of customer demand. This will help you project revenue and estimate profitability. Consider factors such as market size, growth potential, and your competitive position. Utilize forecasting tools and techniques to improve the accuracy of your projections.

- **Expense Management:** Carefully manage your expenses to ensure that they stay within budget and don't erode your profit margins. This involves tracking expenses regularly, identifying areas for cost reduction, and implementing cost-saving measures wherever possible. Consider using budgeting and expense tracking software to monitor your spending and identify areas for improvement.

- **Break-Even Analysis:** Conduct a break-even analysis to determine the minimum sales volume required to cover your fixed and variable costs. This will help you assess the financial viability of your SBU and set realistic sales targets. The break-even point can be calculated by dividing your total fixed costs by your contribution margin (selling price per unit minus variable cost per unit).

- **Sensitivity Analysis:** Perform a sensitivity analysis to understand how changes in key variables, such as sales volume, pricing, or costs, can impact your profitability. This will help you identify potential risks and develop contingency plans. Sensitivity analysis involves creating different scenarios and evaluating their impact on your financial projections.

By clearly defining your profitability goals and tracking your performance against them, you can ensure that your SBU is on track to achieve success and contribute to the overall growth of your company. Regular financial reviews and performance evaluations will help you identify areas for improvement and make necessary adjustments to your strategy.

The GE Strategic Business Unit

GE Matrix	Business Strength		
	Strong	Average	Weak
High	SBU: Successful		
Average		SBU: Average	
Low			SBU: Poor

(Industry Uniqueness on the vertical axis)

Conclusion: Charting New Territories with Confidence

The decision to launch a strategic business unit is a significant one, requiring careful consideration of various factors, including market potential, resource allocation, and strategic alignment. By conducting thorough market research, clearly defining the opportunity, understanding customer needs, analyzing costs, and setting realistic profitability goals, businesses can make informed decisions about whether to embark on this new venture.

Remember, the success of an SBU hinges not on the size of the parent company but on the strength of the opportunity, the quality of the execution, and the ability to adapt to the unique challenges and dynamics of the new market. By approaching this decision with a strategic mindset and a willingness to invest in the necessary resources and capabilities, businesses can unlock new avenues for growth and achieve long-term success.

Launching an SBU is not a guaranteed path to success, but with careful planning, diligent execution, and a focus on customer value, it can be a powerful tool for expanding your business horizons and achieving sustainable growth. By following the roadmap outlined in this chapter and continuously evaluating and adapting your strategies, you can navigate the complexities of the new market with confidence and position your SBU for long-term prosperity.

Chapter 18: B2B Restocking Fees: Three Simple Steps to Covering Carrying Costs

In the dynamic world of B2B transactions, the issue of product returns can often lead to a complex financial dance, leaving vendors grappling with the challenge of balancing customer satisfaction with profitability. Unlike the consumer market, where lenient return policies are the norm, the B2B landscape operates under different dynamics. The products are often customized, the sales cycles are longer, and the financial stakes are considerably higher. Accepting returns without any financial repercussions can significantly impact a company's bottom line, tying up valuable resources and creating logistical challenges.

It's essential to recognize that accepting a product return isn't simply about placing the item back on the shelf. It triggers a series of costs that can quietly erode profit margins. These costs extend beyond the immediate expense of handling and restocking the returned product. They delve into the realm of inventory carrying costs, which encompass a wide array of expenses incurred from the moment a product enters your warehouse until it's sold.

Therefore, it's imperative for businesses to understand that restocking fees are not just about recouping the direct costs of processing returns. They also serve as a mechanism to account for the often-overlooked carrying costs associated with holding inventory. These carrying costs, which include expenses related to storage, capital, obsolescence, and more, can significantly impact a company's profitability, especially in the B2B context where products may have longer shelf lives and higher values.

The Role of Overhead in B2B Restocking Fees

Every company understands that its inventory costs money, but not all are aware of the full extent of these costs or the role that overhead plays. Overhead, often referred to as indirect costs, encompasses all the support functions that enable a business to operate, including sales, marketing, customer service, procurement, accounting, and more. While these functions might not be directly involved in the production of goods, they play a crucial role in managing inventory, generating sales, and ultimately, driving profitability.

Therefore, when a product is returned, it's not just the direct costs of handling and restocking that need to be considered. A portion of the company's overhead should also be factored into the restocking fee to account for the indirect costs associated with managing and selling that inventory. This ensures that the restocking fee accurately reflects the true cost of accepting the return and helps protect the company's profit margins.

Calculating B2B Restocking Fees: A Three-Step Approach

Our approach to determining restocking fees focuses on three key cost drivers: 1) inventory carrying costs, 2) costs of freight (if included as a service), and 3) a portion of overhead to cover support costs. Let's break down each step in detail.

1. **Inventory Carrying Costs:** Most companies apply a standard 3% monthly carrying cost to their inventory value. These costs encompass a range of expenses, including obsolescence, damage, financing, freight, warehouse management, theft, and overtime. The most crucial aspect of our calculation is to cover the time your company holds inventory before it's sold, reflected in your inventory turnover rate.

We'll apply this 3% monthly carrying cost directly to the product's cost of goods sold (COGS) and determine the total carrying costs by considering the number of days the inventory was held before being sold. This covers our original carrying costs. However, we'll double this amount to account for the additional carrying costs incurred when the product is returned and held in inventory again until it's resold. The formula for this step would look like this:

[(Carrying Cost} * Company Overhead Percentage)]

The B2B Restocking Fee Calculation

Fee: {(Initial Carrying Costs) + (New Carrying Costs) + (Per-Unit or Total Freight Cost) + [(Carrying Cost * Company Overhead Percentage)]}

2.   **Costs of Freight:** Inbound freight costs, those associated with getting products into your warehouse, are typically included in the product's COGS and thus not factored into the restocking fee. However, if your company includes freight as a service on delivery, you have the right to recoup this cost when a product is returned.

You can decide whether to include a surcharge on this freight cost. Since you initially provided a delivered price to your customer, and they now wish to return the product, it's reasonable to recoup that original cost. If you also cover the freight cost for the return shipment, that should be factored into the restocking fee as well.

- Freight Cost = Original Outbound Freight Cost + Return Freight Cost (if applicable)

3. **Overhead:** To cover your operational support costs, we'll use your company's overhead percentage in our calculation. This percentage is derived by dividing your indirect expenses (support costs not directly tied to production) by your direct expenses (costs directly linked to manufacturing a product, such as material and labor costs).

In essence, this step ensures that the restocking fee accounts for the portion of your overhead that supported the management and sale of the returned inventory. It recognizes that various departments, such as sales, marketing, customer service, and accounting, play a role in the overall inventory management process, and their costs should be factored into the restocking fee.

- Overhead Cost = Total Carrying Costs * Company Overhead Percentage

The B2B Restocking Fee Calculation

Bringing it all together, the B2B restocking fee can be calculated as follows:

Fee = Total Carrying Costs + Freight Cost + Overhead Cost

Illustrative Example

Let's consider a scenario where a company has a product with a COGS of $1,000. The product was held in inventory for 15 days before being sold, and the company estimates it will take another 15 days to resell it after the return. The company incurred a $30 shipping cost to deliver the product initially, and their current overhead percentage is 50%.

Assuming a 3% monthly carrying cost, let's calculate the restocking fee.

First, we calculate the initial carrying cost:

- Initial Carrying Costs = ($1000 * 0.03 * 15) / 365 = $1.23

Since we're assuming it will take the same amount of time to resell the product, the new carrying costs are also $1.23.

- New Carrying Costs = $1.23

- Total Carrying Costs = $1.23 + $1.23 = $2.46

Next, we factor in the freight cost:

- Freight Cost = $30 (original outbound freight)

Finally, we calculate the overhead cost:

- Overhead Cost = $2.46 * 0.50 = $1.23

Now, let's plug these values into the restocking fee formula:

Fee = $2.46 + $30 + $1.23

Restocking Fee = $33.69

In this example, the restocking fee of $33.69 represents approximately 3.37% of the product's COGS. This fee covers the initial and new carrying costs, the original shipping cost, and a portion of the company's overhead.

The Dangers of Charging a Flat Fee

Some businesses opt for a simpler approach, charging a flat restocking fee of 15% to 20% across all product lines. However, this approach can be detrimental, as it penalizes all customers equally, regardless of the product's inventory turnover rate. Products that sell quickly incur lower carrying costs, so a flat fee might overcharge customers who return such items, potentially damaging customer relationships.

It's crucial to adopt a more nuanced approach that reflects the true costs associated with each product return. By considering factors like inventory turnover rates, carrying costs, freight expenses, and overhead, you can calculate a restocking fee that is both fair to the customer and protects your company's profitability.

Key Principles for Effective Restocking Fees:

1. **Fees Should Reflect Inventory Turnover Rates:** Charge lower fees for products with high turnover rates (sell quickly) and higher fees for products with low turnover rates (take longer to sell). This ensures that the fee is proportionate to the actual carrying costs incurred.

2. **Fees Should Cover Inventory Carrying Costs:** The restocking fee should adequately cover both the initial carrying costs incurred before the sale and the new carrying costs associated with holding the returned item until it's resold.

3. **Fees Should Cover Support Costs:** Include a portion of your company's overhead in the restocking fee to account for

the indirect costs of sales, marketing, customer service, and other support functions that contribute to inventory management and sales. These are support costs that your company should cover within its fees for returned product.

Transparency and Communication: Building Trust with Customers

Be transparent with your customers about your restocking fee policy and calculation method. Explain the rationale behind the fees and how they help offset the costs associated with processing returns. This transparency can foster trust and understanding, reducing the likelihood of disputes or negative customer experiences.

Categorizing Products Based on Turnover Rates: A Tailored Approach

To further refine your restocking fee strategy, consider categorizing your products based on their inventory turnover rates. This allows you to apply different fee structures to different product categories, ensuring that the fees accurately reflect the carrying costs associated with each product type. For example, products with high turnover rates might incur a lower restocking fee, while those with low turnover rates might warrant a higher fee.

Technology and Automation: Streamlining the Returns Process

Technology can play a crucial role in streamlining the returns process and automating restocking fee calculations. Inventory management software and ERP systems can track returned items, calculate restocking fees based on predefined rules, and generate invoices or credit memos automatically. This not only saves time and reduces administrative overhead but also ensures consistency and accuracy in applying restocking fees.

Furthermore, technology can help identify patterns in returns, such as frequent returns from specific customers or product categories. This information can be used to proactively address underlying issues, such as product quality problems or inadequate customer training, and reduce the overall volume of returns. By leveraging data analytics and predictive modeling, businesses can gain insights into return trends and take preventive measures to minimize their impact on profitability.

The Customer Perspective: Addressing Concerns and Objections

While restocking fees can be a valuable tool for businesses, it's important to acknowledge the customer's perspective. Some customers might view restocking fees as unfair or punitive, especially if they're accustomed to the lenient return policies prevalent in the B2C market.

To address these concerns, it's crucial to:

- **Emphasize the Value:** Clearly communicate the value your company provides and the costs associated with processing returns. Explain how restocking fees help cover these costs and ensure that your business remains profitable, allowing you to continue providing high-quality products and services. Highlight the specialized nature of B2B products and the additional costs associated with customization, longer lead times, and potential obsolescence.

- **Offer Alternatives:** In some cases, it might be beneficial to offer alternative solutions to restocking fees, such as store credit or exchanges. This can help maintain customer satisfaction and encourage future purchases. Consider offering flexible return options for valued customers or in situations where the return is due to a product defect or error on your part.

- **Be Flexible:** While it's important to have a clear and consistent return policy, be willing to negotiate restocking fees in certain situations. This demonstrates goodwill and fosters a positive customer relationship. Consider factors such as the customer's history, the reason for the return, and the potential for future business when deciding whether to negotiate.

- **Educate Customers:** Proactively educate customers about your return and restocking fee policies. This can help set clear expectations and reduce the likelihood of disputes or negative experiences. Provide clear and concise information on your website, invoices, and other relevant documents, and be prepared to answer any questions customers might have.

By addressing customer concerns and demonstrating a willingness to work with them, you can maintain positive relationships while still protecting your company's profitability. Remember, customer satisfaction and loyalty are invaluable assets in the B2B marketplace.

Conclusion: A Balanced Approach to Returns Management

Managing product returns in the B2B marketplace is a complex and multifaceted challenge. While it's important to be accommodating to customers, it's equally crucial to protect your company's profitability. Restocking fees can be a valuable tool for achieving this balance, but they should be implemented strategically and with clear communication.

By understanding the unique challenges of B2B returns, accurately calculating restocking fees, and being willing to negotiate when appropriate, businesses can manage returns effectively while maintaining positive customer relationships. Remember, the goal is not to penalize customers but to ensure that the costs associated with returns are fairly shared and that your business remains profitable.

In conclusion, adopting a balanced approach to returns management involves:

- **Clear Policies:** Establish clear and transparent return and restocking fee policies that are readily available to customers. Include these policies on your website, invoices, and other relevant documents, ensuring that customers understand the terms and conditions of returns before making a purchase.

- **Accurate Costing:** Calculate restocking fees based on the actual costs associated with processing and restocking returned items. Avoid arbitrary flat fees and instead use a transparent calculation method that reflects the true cost of handling returns.

- **Flexibility and Negotiation:** Be willing to negotiate restocking fees in certain situations to maintain customer relationships and foster loyalty. Consider offering alternatives like store credit or exchanges, especially for valuable customers or when the return is due to a product defect or error on your part.

- **Technology and Automation:** Leverage technology to streamline the returns process and automate restocking fee calculations. Inventory management software and ERP systems can track returned items, calculate fees based on predefined rules, and generate invoices or credit memos automatically.

- **Customer Communication:** Prioritize clear and proactive communication with customers regarding your return and restocking fee policies. Explain the rationale behind the fees and how they help offset the costs associated with processing returns. Foster open communication and a willingness to work with customers to find mutually agreeable solutions.

In the ever-evolving B2B landscape, where customer expectations are high and competition is fierce, a well-defined and strategically implemented restocking fee policy can be a valuable tool for balancing customer service and financial prudence. It's a testament to a company's commitment to both its customers and its bottom line, ensuring that the costs of returns are fairly shared and that the business remains on a path towards sustainable growth and profitability.